Partnering
in Europe

Incentive Based
Alliancing for Projects

Bob Scott

Published by Thomas Telford Publishing, Thomas Telford Ltd,
1 Heron Quay, London E14 4JD. URL: www.thomastelford.com

Distributors for Thomas Telford books are
USA: ASCE Press, 1801 Alexander Bell Drive, Reston, VA 20191–4400
Japan: Maruzen Co. Ltd, Book Department, 3–10 Nihonbashi 2-chome, Chuo-ku, Tokyo 103
Australia: DA Books and Journals, 648 Whitehorse Road, Mitcham 3132, Victoria

First published 2001

Also available from Thomas Telford Books

Total project management of construction safety, health and environment, ISBN 0 7277 2082 1

Partnering in the social housing sector, ISBN 0 7277 2951 9

The ECI guide to managing health in construction, ISBN 0 7277 2762 1

A catalogue record for this book is available from the British Library

ISBN: 0 7277 2965 9

© Thomas Telford Ltd, 2001

Typeset by Kneath Associates, Swansea

Printed and bound in Great Britain by Hobbs the Printers, Hampshire

Contents

Foreword

The European Construction Institute (ECI) was founded in 1990 to provide a forum for some of the largest, most prestigious clients, contractors and project support organisations in Europe to work together.

The ECI's vision is to create and maintain a globally competitive industry in Europe for the execution of major engineering and construction projects. This goal is underpinned by our mission to align the major supply-chain contributors and collectively devise techniques to improve performance, share experiences of implementation and find common solutions to common problems.

The delivery of the ECI's mission centres on task forces which draw together experts from member companies and the academic community to address those issues our members have identified as crucial to more successful project execution.

The ECI has probably done more work on partnering than any other comparable body in Europe. Starting with the groundbreaking *Contracting Without Conflict* of 1989 which was written by two of the ECI team leaders, this effort continued with *Partnering in the Public Sector*, which was developed to support Sir Michael Latham's work to transform the performance of the UK construction industry, *Partnering in the Social Housing Sector* and this volume. It has also included various seminars and workshops dealing with specific partnering issues and with the requirements of the European procurement rules.

It gives me great pleasure to present the new report of ECI's task force *Partnering in Europe: Incentive Based Alliancing for Projects*. This report focuses on project-specific alliancing and is built on current best practice. More than 40 ECI members have made their contribution, by putting in their ideas and practical experience. We hope that this report will give you, the reader, a tool for a new approach of working together in a world of accelerated change in order to reach our common goal: increased competitiveness of our industry.

Manfred Schlösser
Chairman, ECI

Acknowledgements
(Task Force 23)

The ECI wishes to acknowledge the special contribution of Bob Scott, Chairman of the Task Force and principal author of this report, who in turn wishes to acknowledge the particular contribution of Imre Csoti.

Leaders of the Core Groups

The leaders of the Core Groups, who were responsible for drawing together the material relating to their special interests, were:

Francois Dalla Vecchia

Antonello Furcas

Joseph Infante

Sally Roe

Alan Solomons

Brierley Stubbs.

Members of the Editing Group

The members of the Editing Group, who were responsible for reducing the contributions of the Core Group into a manageable draft document, were:

James Barlow

Imre Csoti

Jean-Luc Heynderickx

Manfred Schlösser

Ivor Williams.

We also acknowledge the support given to Bob Scott by BP/Amoco to enable him to complete this work following his retirement from the company.

This document is dedicated to the memory of Francois Dalla Vecchia.

Task Force Members

APP Consultants   Bob Scott (Chairman)

Agip Eni   Emilio Sonson

AHI Bau Gmbh   Wolfgang McNichols

Alstec Ltd   Martin Austick

AMEC   Tony Green

Applied Project Research   Bob Loraine

BG Transco   Mary Mitchell

BNFL   Tom Carr

Brink Advocates   Mr A. Th. P. A. Brink

Currie & Brown   Jim Stewart and Alan Curtis

Dortmund University   Thomas Shriek

Droege & Company   Samir Jajjawi

ECI   Ivor Williams

Elf   Alain Pierru

EPCI   Bjorn Asbjornslett

Fabricom   Jean-Luc Heynderickx

Faithful & Gould   Brierley Stubbs

Feddersen Laule Scherzberg & Ohle Hansen Ewerwahn   Dr Ekkehard Moeser MCL

Fluor Daniel   Jan Barnhoorn

Foster Wheeler   Alan Solomons

Franklin & Andrews   Jon Jackson

Freshfields Bruckhaus Deringer   Sally Roe

Hertel UK   Stephen R. Tonks

Kingsfield Group   Jerry Lee

Lurgi   Dr Armin Franke

M. W. Kellogg   Paul Larkin

Loughborough University   Professor Geoffrey Trimble

Masons   Mark Lane

Innogy   Charles Tasker

Northcroft   Joseph A. Infante

Ove Arup   Clare Courtney

Parsons   Mike Pearce

Polytechnic of Milan   Corrado Baldi

Ponticelli Freres   F. Dalla Vecchia

Washington Group International   Imre Csoti

Siemens   Carsten Nickelsen

Snamprogetti SpA   Antonello Furcas

SPRU, University of Sussex   Dr James Barlow

STRABAG AG   Manfred Schlösser

Tarmac Construction Services   Shonagh Hay

Technip   Michel Berthon

Weidleplan Consulting Projektmanagement Gmbh   Professor Klaus Roessner

The ECI

To learn more about the European Construction Institute (ECI), its members and work, contact the ECI at the address below or visit the ECI website at http://www.eci-online.org.uk

ECI
Sir Frank Gibb Annex
West Park
Loughborough University
Loughborough
Leicestershire
LE11 3TU

Executive summary

By not daring to take the risk of making the new happen, management takes, by default, the greater risk of being surprised by what will happen. This is the risk that even the largest and richest company cannot afford to take. **Peter Drucker**

It is assumed that your decision to pick up and start reading this book has been prompted by an interest in the subject matter. It may be that you and your company are already practising a form of what has come to be known as 'partnering'. Perhaps you have been aware of the concept for some time but for whatever reason have not felt the need to adopt it. You may even feel that it carries too much risk. Or it may simply be that you have not had an opportunity to do so. For others the concept will be entirely new.

You are probably also reading this because you have an interest in improving your own and your company's performance, from both a financial and a technical perspective, in executing construction projects. Owner companies have to live with the consequences of their projects for many years after they have been brought into operation. So they have a direct interest in the efficiency with which projects are conceived, defined and executed, as this will inevitably, and often significantly, impact on business results over a long period. *Achieving performance improvement is the principal objective of partnering.*

This book is intended primarily for those who have yet to embrace the concept of partnering. Nevertheless, the Task Force hopes and believes that all readers will find something of direct and useful application in improving business performance in a significant way.

Partnering has been finding successful application in the construction industry for at least a decade. Originating in the USA, it has subsequently been widely adopted in the UK and, increasingly, in many other parts of the world, including mainland Europe. The concept of partnering grew out of the realisation that traditional forms of contracting for construction projects were frequently failing to deliver results that were acceptable to either or both the owners and construction contractors. Many reasons for this failure have been put forward, each of which has some degree of validity.

Some failures undoubtedly have had their roots in a simple failure to apply good project-management practices. Indeed, it is worth stating at the outset that *partnering is not, and never will be, a substitute for sound project management*. On the contrary, partnering is unlikely to be effective if this is missing.

Other failures have been related more directly to breakdowns in the relationships between owners and construction contractors. The most common observation has been of an increasing tendency for disputes and even litigation between the parties when problems arise during the course of a project. Such disputes have often proven to be time consuming and costly, and frequently neither party has been satisfied with the outcome. Indeed, it has been noted that the resources devoted to dealing with disputes arising from this so-called *adversarialism* have greatly exceeded those that have or could have been applied to finding effective and mutually acceptable solutions to the original problems.

Partnering takes many forms, but all seek to address the issue of adversarialism directly. It is based on the simple, some would say common sense, premise that **better results can be achieved for all participating companies if they work together towards agreed common goals rather than as individual companies each with its own separate agenda and objectives.**

Of course, many, if not all, projects start with such ideals. The difference with partnering is that it is underpinned with

- contract structures and conditions
- processes
- procedures

specifically designed to generate and, more importantly, sustain genuine alignment between the contracting parties and to secure the commitment of the parties to these ideals, both at a corporate and at an individual level.

This book deals primarily with one project-specific form of partnering which has been found to be particularly effective for specific projects. To distinguish it from other forms of partnering it has been termed *alliancing*. Among the key distinguishing features of alliancing are:

- Key contractors are selected and involved at a very early stage of the project development (usually before the project has received final approval by the owner).
- A 'single project team' is created, comprising the key contractors and the owner.
- The owner is an integral and active member of the *alliance*.

■ The owner and each alliance contractor retain individual corporate accountability, as well as legal rights and obligations, via individual contracts.

■ A financial incentive scheme directly links the rewards of all alliance members to the *overall* outcome of the project rather than just to their individual performance. In many instances the financial incentive scheme is embodied in a separate legal contract or *alliance agreement*.

Not all forms of partnering incorporate a financial incentive scheme to reward all the parties in line with the performance achieved. However, it is a major assertion of the Task Force that the adversarialism referred to earlier can be traced clearly and directly to a lack of commercial alignment between the parties. The financial incentive scheme is designed with the prime purpose of creating and promoting commercial alignment between the parties. Consequently it is considered to be a critical element.

The Task Force also believes that achieving commercial alignment is a key factor in:

■ gaining the true commitment of senior managers
■ eliminating the adversarialism referred to earlier
■ driving the changes in behaviour at the working project level that are considered to be essential to achieving success
■ driving innovation in conceiving and executing projects.

It is recognised that many owners will be doubtful about their ability directly to influence project outcomes. This may well be linked to an ingrained belief that the market and so-called 'competitive bidding' will deliver the right price. Partnering is often also perceived to preclude competition, but this need not, and should not, be the case albeit that contractor selection should be based on factors other than straight commercial considerations.

Partnering, and particularly alliancing, challenges these and other strongly held 'beliefs'. However, when implemented with belief and commitment, significant improvements, and sometimes step changes, in project performance can be achieved as the table on the following page demonstrates.

Partnering may initially be proposed to owners by contractors who have experienced the benefits it can bring. However, there is general agreement that it requires clear and unambiguous leadership and commitment to the approach by the owner if it is to achieve its potential. Alignment across the various parts of the owner's organisation and commitment at the most senior managerial level are considered to be particularly vital. If the potential for performance improvement is to be maximised, it is equally important that alliancing is at the heart of the owner's strategy for the project from the earliest stages.

Project type	Estimated cost 'business as usual' (millions)	Approved investment (sanction) cost[1] (millions)	Actual final cost[2] (millions)
Offshore platform	£450	£373	£290
Refinery revamp	Not known	US $295	US $269
Addition to existing petrochemical plant	US $175	US $49	US $133
Onshore gas terminal	£123	£119	£92
Offshore gas pipeline	£348	£319	£242
Refinery revamps:			
Hydrocracker	Not known	£41	£39
FCCU	Not known	£54	£47

FCCU, Fluidised-bed catalytic cracking unit.

[1]This cost is developed jointly by the owner and the main contractors working together before seeking final investment approval.
[2]Actual cost before sharing of savings.

Capital costs of a variety of alliance projects

The main part of this book (Part 2) takes the form of a 'tool-kit'. It has been developed from the contributions of individuals, most of whom have had direct experience in setting up and working in alliances. It is designed to provide practical guidance in setting up an alliance. However, it is extremely important that alliancing (and indeed any form of partnering) is not seen to be a simple and slavish application of a 'recipe'. Neither should alliancing be regarded simply as an alternative form of contract. Either of these approaches may well lead to disappointment. In view of this it is recommended that the tool-kit be regarded as a practical guide to good practice in creating a successful alliance. Those using it should not hesitate to adapt it as may be considered appropriate to meet their own specific circumstances. In making adaptations, however, care must be exercised to ensure that the fundamental principles are retained.

Contractual aspects are extremely important in providing a solid foundation for a successful alliance, as is the application of sound project-management techniques, processes and procedures. However, as has already been noted, the human aspects of relationships and behaviours are no less important. Alliancing requires investment in people. It can be clearly argued that failure to pay adequate attention to or make an appropriate investment in any of these aspects will greatly diminish the potential of achieving a successful outcome.

Another point of note is that a majority of successful alliances have reported that the use of facilitation and team building for high performance was an extremely important factor in their success. Many indicated that the benefits of this were greatest when external consultants were employed in these areas, with three main reasons being quoted:

- specialist skills and expertise are brought to bear, particularly in the area of creating a high performing team
- good facilitation is necessary to ensure that there is clarity of purpose between owners and contractors
- third parties bring independent views and insights that are extremely helpful in breaking down barriers between the parties.

Finally, the contributors to and author of this book fully appreciate that adopting alliancing may appear to be a daunting task. However, the potential rewards are significant and could have a real impact on your future and that of your company; it is clear to the Task Force that it is the decision to start the process that is the most difficult. Readers should perhaps take comfort in the following quotation:

The distance is nothing; it is only the first step that is difficult.
Mme du Deffand (Marie de Vichy-Chamrond), 18th century French literary hostess.

The Task Force is also confident that all the potential barriers to alliancing, either real or perceived, can be overcome. It sincerely trusts that this book will not only help you to be convinced of that but also, and more importantly, that it will give you the confidence to take that first difficult step and subsequently help and support you in staying the distance and delivering a successful alliancing future.

Introduction

This book is aimed primarily at encouraging the adoption and supporting the ongoing implementation of project-specific partnering – referred to here as 'alliancing' – within the private construction sector in mainland Europe. The word 'project' is intended to cover a wide range of activities, from brand new capital projects through to the refurbishment and/or maintenance of existing facilities. The book is in two parts.

Part 1 begins with a broad definition of partnering and a description of two categories of the concept. Alliancing is distinguished as a specific form of partnering within one of these categories (project-specific partnering) and the key features of an alliance are listed and discussed.

The case for adopting alliancing is then put forward, first by examining the limitations of current or 'traditional' approaches to contracting. The main ways in which alliancing addresses these limitations are outlined and the tangible and intangible benefits are covered. The circumstances in which alliancing will be a suitable approach are then discussed.

Potential barriers to alliancing arising from the way in which companies are organised and from organisational and individual cultural issues are then addressed. Ways in which owners who do not possess project-management skills can still contemplate adopting alliancing are also covered.

Finally, concerns regarding legal implications that are frequently raised by those new to alliancing are examined through looking at the specific implications of current European Union laws and regulations. Approaches complying with current legislation are presented and discussed.

Part 2 is the main part of the book. It is presented as a tool-kit or 'road map' for those wishing to set up an alliance. Each of the sections deals with a specific aspect of creating a successful alliance. It starts by giving an overview of the alliance implementation process, and then proceeds to cover the process of achieving commitment and alignment within the owner's organisation. This is followed by guidance on the selection of alliance contractors and a short section that gives some guidance on how owners approach starting the process with potential alliance contractors.

Possible contract structures for alliancing as well as specific contractual issues are then presented. This draws on specific documents that have been used in a wide range of such arrangements, as well as the experience of personnel who have been directly involved. The alliance incentive scheme is then covered in more detail.

Project organisation and procedures and processes specific to alliancing are looked at in the next two sections. Approaches to building and sustaining effective relationships within an alliance are discussed. Monitoring performance is a key part of sustaining relationships, and this is covered immediately afterwards.

The tool-kit finishes with a section giving guidance on building relationships with supply chains, government, local authority and other statutory bodies and, not least, other external organisations and individuals.

The contents of the tool-kit have been drawn from the direct experience of individuals who participated in the task force and have personal experience of alliancing and partnering in general. It sets out all the major principles that should be taken into account in developing an alliance and ways in which these can be implemented. However, each project will have its own unique set of circumstances and to meet these it will often be necessary to adapt the approaches recommended in the tool-kit. Indeed, the Task Force is strongly of the view that application of the tool-kit as though it were merely a recipe could detract significantly from the chances of achieving the best possible results. Finally, all parties involved in creating an alliance should ensure that they obtain proper legal advice at all appropriate points.

Part 1

Understanding partnering/alliancing

1. What is partnering?

Summary

This section defines partnering in its widest sense for the purposes of this book. The cooperative nature of partnering and its emphasis on improving the delivery of projects is highlighted, as is the way in which it differs from previous forms of cooperation between companies.

Two specific categories of partnering – long term and project specific – are described, and alliancing is distinguished as a particular form. The key features of an alliance are then discussed.

Many of the key features and principles covered will apply to all forms of partnering.

Contents

- **Definition and nature of partnering**

- **Categories of partnering**
  Long term and project specific
  An alliance as a distinct form of project-specific partnering

- **Key features of an alliance**
  Early involvement of alliance participants
  Equitable relationships
  Commitment of senior management
  Commercial alignment
  An integrated team
  – Team organisation
  – Team alignment and commitment
  Trust
  Innovation
  Open communication

1.1 Definition

Many definitions of partnering exist. However, for the purpose of this book it is simply defined as follows:

> Partnering is a relationship between two or more companies or organisations which is formed with the express intent of improving performance in the delivery of projects.

Partnering is designed to achieve specific business objectives and significantly improve the business performance of all the participants through a set of processes and procedures aimed at maximising the effectiveness of their resources – skills, expertise and knowledge. These processes and procedures are designed to enhance the levels of cooperation and collaboration between the partnering companies. They are also designed to generate and sustain alignment between the companies and their commitment to achieving performance improvements.

Partnering is distinguished from other forms of collaborative working (e.g. joint ventures between contractors) in that the owner is always one of the active participating organisations. Partnering requires firms to move from traditional relationships towards a relationship that is based on alignment and commitment to achieving common goals which are in the interests of all the participating companies. In turn this requires a clear understanding of the other party's individual expectations and values, and the creation of an environment in which goodwill, trust, teamwork and innovation can be developed and sustained.

Whatever form partnering takes, it must never be seen as a 'bolt-on' option to the contracting strategy – it should be an integral part of the contracting approach from the earliest phases of project planning.

1.2 Categories of partnering

Typically, partnering falls into two broad categories:

- *Long-term partnering* (sometimes referred to as strategic alliancing). This type of arrangement generally covers the provision of services over a specified period of years and is most commonly between the owner and a single contractor.
- *Project-specific partnering*. This type of arrangement lasts for the duration of a single project. In this instance, the arrangement can be between the owner and a single contractor, but more commonly it is between the owner and several contractors.

A variation of project-specific partnering is where the arrangement is underpinned by an incentive scheme, whereby the rewards of the contractors and, indeed, the owner are linked directly to actual performance during the execution phase of the project. This book deals specifically with this form of project-specific partnering, which is commonly known as alliancing. The terms *alliance* and *alliancing* are used throughout the text. However, most of the material covered in this book applies equally to all forms of partnering.

1.3 Key features of project alliances

Most successful alliances display a number of key features. The most important of these are highlighted in the subsections below, and all of them are dealt with in more detail later in this book.

1.3.1 Early involvement of key participants

The shape and eventual outcome of any project can be most heavily influenced in the early stages of the project's development as Figure 1 illustrates. Early involvement of key project participants (the *alliance members*) allows their expertise

Figure 1

An influence curve for a project

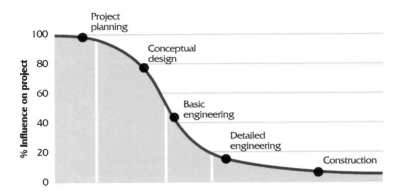

and knowledge to be brought to bear at this crucial stage, resulting in a better defined project and greater certainty regarding its eventual delivery.

Open sharing of best practises in value engineering, together with a focus on design innovation, simplification and optimisation, and constructability at the earliest possible opportunity provides significant potential for reducing project costs and schedules. Apart from these benefits, early selection and involvement means that all the alliance participants have an opportunity to develop other key aspects of successful alliances before project execution starts.

When and how the alliance members should be engaged will depend on the nature of the project. However, the general rule should be to engage them at the earliest possible opportunity. As a minimum, all alliance members should be selected so that they can participate in the formulation of the project-cost estimates and execution schedules, which will form the basis of the owner's final decision to proceed with the project.

It should be emphasised that early selection does not prevent competitive tendering. There is absolutely no reason why the selection process cannot be based on normal so-called 'hard' criteria, such as costs, technical competence, track record, current workload and safety record, as well as so-called 'soft' criteria, such as corporate attitude and culture, personnel attitudes, management and methods.

1.3.2 Equitable relationship

Designing and implementing an equitable win–win relationship is one of the pillars of successful alliancing. This will involve firms developing agreed objectives, as well as finding ways of accommodating each other's individual objectives. A critical hurdle to be overcome in arriving at a successful win–win relationship is that of identifying the risks associated with a project and apportioning these between the parties.

1.3.3 Managerial commitment

The level of commitment of *senior management* in the individual organisations is fundamentally important. Senior personnel frequently play a vital role in introducing and supporting the alliancing concept within their organisation. Selling the concept to those around and below them in the organisation's hierarchy and convincing doubters is critical. Finding individuals who can nurture the alliancing process on a day-to-day basis is also critical. This can be aided by ensuring that all those involved in an alliancing arrangement understand that its goals are mutually agreed, and are not imposed from above or by the owner. Commitment is also important because problems inevitably arise on any project, and if commitment is not present then the tendency to revert to 'traditional' behaviours may well prove irresistible.

The commitment of senior management within the owner's organisation and of the owner's key representative on the project team (the owner's project manager) are of particular importance. The former have a pivotal role to play in creating and sustaining the relationship with their peers in the other alliance participant's organisation, while the owner's project manager plays a similar pivotal role in respect of the project team.

1.3.4 Commercial alignment

Many of the sources of poor performance in traditional contracting approaches can be traced to commercial misalignment between the owner and the contracting companies, and between the different contractors engaged on the same project. This misalignment is generated largely because the owner and the contractors have different commercial interests once contracts have been awarded. In turn, this is principally a result of the emphasis that is placed on selecting contractors solely, or largely, on bid costs.

Alliancing creates commercial alignment by instituting an incentive scheme that firmly links the returns of all the alliance participants to actual performance against specific criteria. These criteria are a direct measure of the overall project outcome rather than just of each contractor's individual performance. The 'targets' for the performance criteria are derived from jointly developed and agreed data, such as project-cost estimates and schedules. It is important that the criteria are regarded by all parties as being achievable. They should not, however, be conservative.

1.3.5 Integrated team

The creation of an effective 'single' integrated project team is crucial to success. There are two aspects to this:

- the organisational structure of the team
- the alignment and commitment of the team members both individually and collectively.

Project team structure

One of the key underpinning concepts of alliancing is that each of the parties retains accountability for delivering the part of the project for which it has been selected (e.g. design, fabrication, construction), but at the same time there is a collective responsibility for delivery of the complete project. The organisational structure of the project must be constructed in such a way that it recognises and demonstrates these two points. The allocation of personnel to the team, and especially to key positions, must reflect individual corporate accountability. Each of the key functional areas (e.g. design, fabrication, construction) of the team should be led by a person from the party that is accountable for that function.

To reflect the collective responsibility of the parties the organisation should be constructed in such a way that it eliminates duplication of functions to the maximum extent possible. Areas where needless duplication can often occur include planning, cost control, procurement and technical and safety audits. The parties should take active steps to determine the extent to which duplication might or does occur and to explore every opportunity for integrating such functions. In doing so care must be taken to ensure that individual corporate needs are met.

Creating an integrated team can bring immediate benefits through a reduction in the manpower resources allocated to the project. It also offers the possibility of other efficiency gains through having single point accountability and more transparent processes than might otherwise be the case.

Figure 2

An example of an integrated team

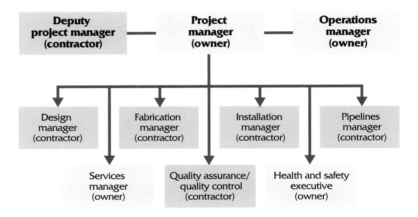

The organisational structure should be jointly developed and endorsed by all the parties. An example of an integrated team structure used on an alliance project is shown in Figure 2.

Project team alignment and commitment

Ultimately, an alliance derives its main power from the effectiveness of the project team. It is widely recognised that it is people and the way in which they work individually and collectively that is the main determinant of the results obtained.

Research has indicated that the performance of a team can be linked to a number key factors, including:

- clear leadership
- team capability
- clarity of roles and responsibilities
- effective communications throughout the team
- understanding of and alignment with project aims
- motivation and commitment to achieve results
- a 'no blame' culture
- recognition and acknowledgement of individual contributions
- arrangements to foster team integration.

All these factors are important and necessary features for a team to be effective. However, it is arguable that in themselves these factors are insufficient, and that the single most important driver of team performance is the strength of the alignment and commitment of the team leaders and team members to achieving results. If this alignment and commitment is sufficiently strong then the team itself is likely to take the actions and put in place processes, procedures and structures that are consistent with delivering the results they want to achieve.

Alignment and commitment is unlikely to occur naturally, and positive action is usually required to engender it. Senior management personnel from all the parties as well as the project manager have an important part to play in this respect. Many successful alliance teams have reported that investing in the use of external consultants with specific skills in this area has played an important, if not indispensable, part in their success.

1.3.6 Trust

The majority of participants in alliances have asserted that trust is an essential element of success, and the importance of trust has been borne out by studies of such arrangements. In considering the question of trust it is important to understand what is meant by the term. The Construction Industry Institute has an accepted definition of 'trust', on which the following definition is based:

> Trust is the confidence and reliance one party has in the professional competence and integrity of the other party (parties) to contribute to the successful execution of a project in a spirit of openness, fairness and cooperation.

It is important that those new to alliancing recognise and acknowledge that trust, in its widest sense, is unlikely to exist at the outset. In reality trust is usually developed and strengthened over time as the alliance participants work with each other. Consequently, the existence of trust should not be viewed as a prerequisite for deciding to adopt alliancing. Initiating alliancing will usually require that the parties make an initial 'leap of faith'. However, such a leap should always be underpinned by evidence that the parties are committed to working together in a way in which trust can rapidly be developed.

Rapid development of trust, is particularly important in the context of projects that usually have relatively short time spans, because it is key to the development of the openness, sharing and commitment to each other which are the hallmarks of, and key to, creating a truly effective and high performing team.

1.3.7 Innovation

Innovative thinking and the application of new approaches, both at a technical level and at an engineering and business process level, drive the achievement of significantly improved performance. Thus creating structures and processes to encourage and promote innovative thinking and application should be a key focus for those participating in an alliance. This must be continuous through all phases of the project, including execution.

Incorporating uncontrolled changes during execution can be a major factor in poor performance. However, if proposals for new ideas and approaches are evaluated via coherent and disciplined processes that take into account the overall project objectives and the interests of the alliance participants, then change can have the entirely opposite effect.

1.3.8 Open communication

Communication is always important, but in an alliance open and honest communication between all the parties is vital. It promotes all the key behavioural aspects of alliancing, and is particularly important in encouraging everyone to confront issues and differences of view from the perspective of developing solutions rather than allowing them to escalate into disputes.

Companies participating in an alliance should also give very careful thought to considering what information can be shared with the others in the alliance. The more information that is relevant to developing the understanding of the others that can be shared the better. In some instances this may include information that individual companies have previously considered to be confidential.

Structures and processes need to be established that will support communication. These should be flexible, and every effort should be made to make information flows as simple as possible. Personal contact between key staff on a day-to-day basis, as well as at regular meetings, is important.

2. Why adopt alliancing?

Summary

This section makes the case for the alliancing approach and should be read by all those to whom the concept is new.

The limitations of traditional contracts are addressed, as is how the built-in misalignment which they create drives each contracting party to achieve their own goals rather than the goals of the project. Since these goals rarely coincide, the misalignment fuels conflict when things do not proceed as planned, and each party attempts to protect its own position. The three main ways in which partnering addresses the limitations of traditional contracting approaches are outlined and the potential benefits discussed.

Headline results from a selection of alliance projects are presented to illustrate the real tangible benefits that can be achieved, and a selection of other intangible benefits that have been reported by participants in alliances are reported.

Finally, the circumstances that best suit an alliancing approach are identified and discussed.

Contents

- **Limitations of traditional contracting**
  Misalignment between owners and contractors
  – Remuneration terms
  – Selection criteria
  Misalignment between contractors
  Lack of access to contractor expertise

- **How alliancing addresses limitations**

- **Alliance benefits**
  Tangible
  Intangible

- **Circumstances suitable for alliancing**
  Owner's business philosophy
  Project size
  Project uncertainties and risk factors
  Contractor availability and capability
  Commercial alignment

- **Summary**

In reality, the only justification for adopting alliancing is the prospect of improvements in the form of specific measures, such as lower costs, faster schedules, better quality and greater certainty, compared with what traditional contracting approaches can deliver. This section presents arguments that traditional approaches to contracting have inherent limitations which inhibit project performance. It then outlines how alliancing is designed to:

- overcome these limitations
- open up the opportunity to improve measurable performance, especially in respect of cost and schedule

- promote a fuller understanding of the risks associated with a project
- reduce the likely impact of these risks
- increase the certainty of the eventual outcome of the project, either by matching or by showing an improvement on the outcome predicted at the time when the owner takes the decision to proceed.

Headline evidence of the improvements in performance that have been achieved by those who have used alliancing is provided in the table in the Executive Summary (see page xv), and an outline is given of some of the other more intangible benefits that have been attributed to the concept. The circumstances in which an alliancing approach would be appropriate are discussed.

2.1 Limitations of 'traditional' contracting

Current practice in contracting has some fundamental limitations which can have a serious impact on project delivery. In order to design a contracting approach that overcomes these limitations it is first necessary to understand what the limitations are and acknowledge that they do exist.

In essence it is postulated that there are three principal areas in which the traditional approach to contracting has limitations:

- misalignment between the owner and the individual contractors
- misalignment between the individual contractors
- lack of access to contractors' skills and expertise at a time when they can best and most influence the eventual outcome.

The reality of traditional contracting is that the schedule and cost targets established prior to project execution almost always escalate upwards. Alliancing offers an approach which affords the opportunity to, at worst, contain cost and schedule overruns and, at best, to achieve lower costs and faster schedules – often substantially so – without sacrificing other important factors such as quality and safety.

2.1.1 Misalignment between owner and contractors

Misalignment between the owner and individual contractors within a project is most often evident in terms of each party's commercial objectives. Almost invariably, contractors are focused on, and are rewarded for, what they achieve in respect of their own part of the project. The owner, on the other hand is primarily concerned with the delivery of the project as a whole. Superficially these two objectives may be aligned, but general experience suggests that real alignment is rare.

Contractors who design and build projects are paid on an individual basis for the work done and have no further interest in the project once their services have been completed. For the contractor, this has two effects:

- their payment is tied to completion of their work only
- they usually have little or no real incentive to design and build the solutions that are economically optimal from the owner's perspective.

Commercial misalignment between owners and contractors is frequently exacerbated by the way in which contractors are remunerated and selected.

Remuneration

A wide variety of remuneration forms are used in traditional contracting. In essence, these are usually located somewhere on the spectrum between full reimbursement of costs and a fixed lump sum.

In a fully cost-reimbursable contract it can clearly be argued that a contractor has little incentive to reduce costs. The contractor is insulated from the effect of cost overruns and is often paid a percentage of its costs to cover overheads and to provide it with profit. The greater the costs incurred, the greater the sums received by the contractor by way of a contribution to overheads and profit. The contractor may even make profit on the contribution to overheads to the extent that the increased contribution exceeds the incremental cost of the additional overhead. This creates an environment where often it is in the contractor's interest to increase expenditure.

At the other end of the spectrum is fixed lump-sum contracting. Here the difficulty is that contractors are asked to quote lump sums on the basis of incomplete data and frequently without a full appreciation of risks. This form of contracting also means that the contractor will bear the complete 'execution risk', and so a prudent contractor will usually include a substantial provision within their quoted price to cover that risk. After contract award the contractor's principal goal will be to protect the profitability of the lump sum. The contractor may also have a tendency to focus on trying to convert the 'risk' provision in the lump sum into profit, either by aiming for greater efficiency or by trying to cut corners.

Various adjustments are frequently introduced to compensate for deficiencies in these various forms of remuneration. Typically these might include various forms of bonuses and penalties. These can help to generate alignment by linking a performance parameter that the owner wishes to achieve to the financial remuneration of the contractor. In cases where these incentives are properly conceived and the contractor has the possibility to earn additional income through good performance there have been positive results.

In many instances, however, the 'incentives' are primarily geared to managing and protecting the owner's risk rather than to promoting improvement in the contractor's performance. For example, the owner might under certain circumstances withhold part of the contractor's normal remuneration. In such cases it is obvious that the one-sided nature of the arrangement is unlikely to be conducive to creating alignment or improving performance.

However successful individual incentive arrangement schemes may be, the fact remains that they are usually only indirectly related to the overall project outcome and the owner's overall objectives. There is also still a significant risk that the owner can end up paying out a substantial incentive payment to an individual contractor or contractors for a project that, in the owner's terms, has been unsuccessful.

Selection criteria

It would be fair to say that in the vast majority of cases cost is the principal, and frequently the sole, criterion for selecting contractors. This is based on the belief that the 'market' will deliver the 'right' price, at least from the point of view of the owner. However, it is evident that this reliance on the market has some deficiencies. What is clear is that the market will deliver the lowest 'bid cost' in line with the market conditions prevalent at the time when bids are sought.

When economic conditions are buoyant and contractors' workloads are high, bid costs will usually reflect this in higher costs. Clearly this is not in the owner's interests. Conversely, when economic conditions are depressed and workloads are low, bid costs are also likely to be low. One or several contractors may even be willing to quote prices at which they would make little or even no profit. While this may appear to be attractive to the owner, the consequences usually are:

- a lack of commitment by the contractor to delivering what is best for the owner
- considerable time and effort being spent by both sides in dealing with commercial issues and disputes arising from the contractor's likely focus on containing losses or increasing his profitability
- cost escalation and late project completion.

The following are two examples of how relying on the market can frustrate attainment of the owner's objectives.

Example 1. Use of a lump-sum-price contract would appear to be appropriate if the project is sufficiently well defined. However, requesting lump sums in a strongly rising market or a location where price escalation is high may be inappropriate, due to the inability of the contract parties to oversee the financial risk they are taking on board (even if escalation formulae are provided). Should the financial situation turn out negatively and the contracting parties run into difficulties or are unprepared to proceed without additional compensation, the owner is likely to be in a poor position even to judge the legitimacy of such claims. Since the owner believes that the transference of such risks to the contractor has already been paid for via the contract price, the parties move inexorably towards litigation.

Example 2. An owner is trying to define the process for a new manufacturing facility and requests a lump-sum price for engineering services for the definition phase of the work. The contractor considers a limited number of alternatives and proposes a process scheme that subsequently proves to have high operating costs and uses technology that is going to be superseded. Here the contracting strategy does not fit with the structure of the project. The contractor has no incentive to explore and push the boundaries of possibility, since in helping the owner he is likely to lose money. Consequently, the owner has defined a project that will perform as an also-ran in the marketplace, which will harm the long-term future of the business.

2.1.2 Misalignment between contractors

Traditional contracting structures frequently create misalignment between the individual contractors. This is because each contractor has a financial interest only in its own performance and has no incentive to work in a way that is most efficient for the project as a whole or to work proactively (by pooling skills, expertise and resources if appropriate) with other contractors and achieve overall efficiency. In reality the opposite usually applies. Individual contractors often see an opportunity to gain from inefficiency and confusion at the interfaces by instituting claims (often perfectly valid) that their ability to perform their contractual obligations has been adversely affected by the failure of others to perform.

The owner's response to this has been either to:

- assume responsibility for interface management, or
- utilise a single contracting organisation in the belief that this reduces the interfaces.

The first of these responses usually requires the dedication of a large and costly team of personnel, whose role is largely that of containing risk rather than of proactively seeking to add value.

The second response may permit more effective management, but the interfaces still exist and the only real difference is that they are less transparent to the owner. Using a single contractor also means that the owner is confined to selecting the contractor that is considered the best in overall terms rather than a group of contractors each of which is considered the best in a particular area of expertise or service.

2.1.3 Lack of access to contractor expertise

The traditional approach to contracting means that, even if they are recognised, the strengths and expertise of contractors are rarely effectively utilised by the owner. In part, this stems from the legacy of large centralised engineering departments and a culture in which contractors and suppliers are largely expected to do as they are told and are subject to heavy levels of monitoring and supervision by the owner. It also in part emanates from a fear of owners that engaging and committing to contractors before the project is fully or sufficiently defined will leave them commercially exposed.

The result of this approach is that it is quite normal not to involve the full range of key contractors until the design and definition of the key features of the project have been fixed and the owner has given final approval for the project to proceed. This happens despite it being widely recognised that this precludes access to the skills and expertise of these contractors at a time when they could most influence the overall optimisation of the design of the facilities and ensure that designs will be able to benefit from taking advantage of their specific infrastructure and methods of working.

Apart from losing the contractors' ability to contribute to producing an optimum project design, failure to engage key contractors at a sufficiently early stage also carries other potential penalties for the owner, including the following:

- Cost estimates will be more uncertain than they need be. This is always important, but particularly so if, as frequently occurs, the owner makes an investment decision prior to approaching the market. Thus the cost estimates are more uncertain simply because a lower proportion of the total cost is 'committed'.
- Project execution schedules will carry more uncertainty. Because the key contractors will have had no input, the schedules will be inherently more uncertain. Owners tend to deal with this by imposing a schedule on contractors, but even if this works insofar as the schedule is concerned it is often at the expense of a higher cost.
- The total risk profile of the project is less well understood than it could otherwise be. Experience clearly indicates that contractors can make a significant contribution to developing a more comprehensive understanding of the risks associated with a particular project.

2.2 How does alliancing address the limitations of current practice?

Very simply, alliancing addresses the shortcomings of traditional contracting by:

- Identifying, selecting and involving all the key contractors (and sometimes the vendors of major equipment) at an early stage of the project development, usually for the front-end engineering development (FEED) immediately prior to owner sanction for the project being sought.
- Affording the contractors a genuine opportunity to work together and with the owner to:
  - design and define the most appropriate and economic project
  - jointly develop cost estimates and project schedules before the owner gives final approval to proceed with the project
  - identify all the risks associated with the project and design management, and

mitigation measures for these

– clarify and define the specific responsibilities and accountabilities of each of the participants and the interfaces between them.

■ Creating commercial alignment by giving the contractors a direct financial stake in the efficient design and execution of the project via an incentive scheme that is based on criteria directly linked to the overall outcomes.

All of the above results in a project with greater certainty of outcome for all the participants. One particularly striking aspect is that all the participants, including the contractors, now have a direct interest in ensuring that the interfaces between them are managed efficiently.

Figure 3 and Table 1 show, respectively, the essential differences in the way project costs accumulate and benefits are distributed in a traditional fixed lump-sum environment and an alliance environment.

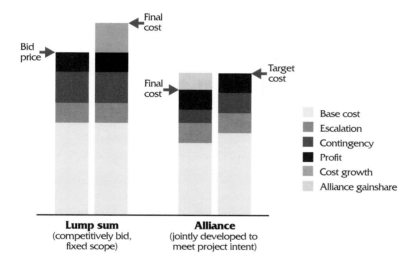

Figure 3

The development of costs in a lump-sum and an alliance environment

Benefit	Lump sum	Alliance (reimbursable/target price)
Purchased materials		
Material cost savings	C	P
Manufacturing efficiency savings	C	P
Installed quantity savings	C	P
Field labour costs		
Labour efficiency improvement	C	P
Labour cost savings	C	P
Installed quantity savings	C	P
Other aspects		
Schedule improvements	C	P
Potential for claims	+ +	– –
Incentives possible	Sch/Op/Sa/Q	Co/Sch/Op/Sa/Q
Commercial alignment mechanism	None/contract	Target price + criteria
Contingency approach	Blind	Open
Profit approach	Blind	Open
Post-contract change	Difficult and/or costly	Flexible

C, contractor; Co, cost; Op, operability; P, alliance partners; Q, quality; Sa, safety; Sch, schedule.

Table 1

The distribution of benefits in a lump-sum and an alliance environment

2.3 Alliance benefits

The benefits of alliancing can be classified into two broad categories:

■ Tangible benefits, which are clear and directly measurable (e.g. cost reduction and faster implementation schedules).

■ Intangible benefits, which either cannot be measured, are difficult to measure with precision or are not directly measurable, but which are likely or may contribute to achieving future tangible benefits.

2.3.1 Tangible benefits

The most powerful reason for adopting an alliancing approach is that it has produced some extremely good results for both owners and contractors. A selection of capital cost results achieved on a variety of projects is given in the table in the Introduction to this book.

2.3.2 Intangible benefits

Intangible benefits reported by owners, contractors and their personnel involved in alliance projects include:

■ Enhanced practices, processes and procedures that are transferable to future projects, even those that are not alliances.

■ Rationalised and streamlined project procedures have led to a simpler organisation and reduced resource requirement.

■ Employees have learned communication skills and problem-solving mechanisms which will be of help in their future work, even outside an alliance.

■ Learning from alliance working has improved overall company competitiveness.

■ Employees are more motivated and more focused on performance improvement.

■ Employees are much happier in their work.

■ The creation of an environment where skills, expertise and knowledge are valued has allowed individuals at all levels to make a positive contribution and to achieve self-development.

■ The company reputation and profile has been enhanced.

■ The development of a longer term business relationship from an initial one-off alliance.

■ A much better understanding has been achieved of the totality of the risks associated with projects and how to manage these more effectively.

2.4 Circumstances suitable for alliancing

There are clearly differences between European countries in the way the construction industry is organised and in the problems it faces. However, in today's world performance improvement is an imperative not just for owners but equally for contractors and suppliers, both across Europe and elsewhere. Minimising cost and time inflation, maximising quality and improving safety standards are key objectives for all involved in the construction industry.

More fundamentally, traditional approaches to the construction process are becoming less suitable for fulfilling the demands of certain types of project. Many projects are growing in technical complexity, value and risk. Some also involve an element of flexibility in project ends and means. Under these circumstances it becomes critical to coordinate the large number of specialist participants that are often involved. It is considered that alliancing has particular application in projects that have these characteristics. The early involvement of all key parties enables greatly improved project planning and design at the front end, and thus increases certainty of delivery.

However, there are a number of factors that could influence the decision to adopt an alliancing approach, and some of these are discussed below. These factors are not presented as a checklist or recipe to be followed, but rather to give an insight into circumstances that would favour the adoption of alliancing and thus help in the decision-making process in individual cases.

2.4.1 Owner business philosophy

If alliancing is viewed as a non-traditional approach to contracting for major projects, then the question arises as to why an owner may or may not desire to explore such an approach. The premise here is that there are different approaches to business performance and, depending on an owner's value orientation, a different view on life will result. To illustrate this point three categories are proposed: business as usual, continuous improvement and breakthrough performance.

Business as usual

This is characterised by the view that: 'Marketplace knowledge and processes bring sufficient value to what I want to do'.

Contract forms that spring to mind here are traditional lump-sum turn-key (LSTK) and lump-sum services type contracts. With these contract forms the requirements are clearly defined at the bid invitation stage, and once competitively bid and awarded the parties are essentially prisoner to what they have agreed to. These contract types are in wide use and have delivered successful projects all over the world.

Continuous improvement

This is characterised by the view that: 'I am interested in innovation and new ways of doing things, however incremental change is the preferred way'.

Here contracts contain incentives. A typical incentive is where a portion of the contractor's remuneration is linked to the performance of the project. The performance parameters are normally defined by the owner in the beginning, and the onus is on the contractor to deliver the agreed parameters and thus to recover his full profit margin.

Breakthrough performance

This is characterised by the view that: 'I am dissatisfied with capital project and business venture performance and require increased value from investments'.

The owner looking for breakthrough performance will recognise that a new approach is required and that a number of barriers to superior performance exist with traditional contract forms. Alliancing as a concept is likely to be of most interest to this category of owners and of some interest those who are principally looking for incremental performance gains.

2.4.2 Project size

If an organisation is searching for improved performance through project execution, then the potential benefits to be realised should also be substantial, since the success of the capital investment programme of a business will determine the organisation's overall success for a long time in the future.

Investing in a change initiative of this type also requires the allocation of skilled personnel. So the project size does play a role, in that there should be a reasonable expectation that the benefits should be recoverable on that particular project since investment plans for the future are always uncertain. It is recognised, however, that for some owners who are starting the process this might not be a main consideration. Using a smaller project as a learning test bed before applying the concept to larger projects may be more important to some owners than gaining immediate benefits.

A small-scale survey of owners in the process industries suggested that most owners would consider projects below about £15–20 million as not being ideal. However, the concept has been successfully used on projects with values as low as about £10 million and as high as £1000 million or more.

2.4.3 Project uncertainty and risk factors

A large number of variables determine the level of risk of a project. Risk can be seen as accruing from complexity (many projects today are complex by definition), scale (largest of a kind), technology (first of a kind), location (new for the owner and/or the contracting companies), schedule requirements (shorter than previously achieved) and cost (desire for better than historical preference). These macro-risk factors can occur alone or in combination.

Alliances are powerful risk-mitigating organisations because, not only are they able to analyse better the true risks of realising the project, but also they are better set up to deal with the consequences. There is no interest in merely transferring risk to another party, since the risk is shared from the beginning with the owner. The important task is to analyse the risks and identify the party best able to control them.

Complexity is a major factor in increasing the risk of conventional projects. For example, revamp and de-bottlenecking projects, which comprise the need to carry out major modifications while existing facilities remain in operation and the need to bring new systems into operation on a piecemeal basis, increase the project-management complexity enormously. Figure 4 shows one view of the use of alliance contracts in relation to the complexity of the business and the culture of the owner–contractor relationships.

Figure 4

Contract strategy versus complexity and challenge

Traditional contract forms tend to reach their limitations or break down completely as business complexity increases. This leaves two choices:

- simplify the business (e.g. by breaking the project up into its component parts, by ensuring a high level of definition prior to contracting)
- change the culture of the business environment (alliancing is a way of achieving this).

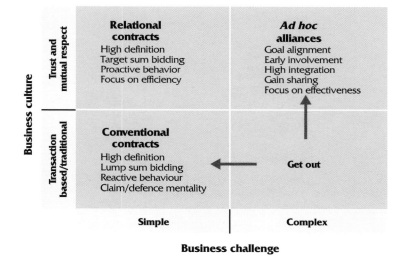

2.4.4 Alliance partner (contractor) availability and capability

It is important that the contractors selected as alliance partners are those who are best placed to share the risk associated with the specific project circumstances. Since the alliance partners are being asked to commit to share the overall risk through the financial incentive scheme, a commitment by a contractor needs to be backed up by an ability to bear financial risk.

When qualified companies with the required skills or resources are limited in number, there is an especially strong reason to consider an alliancing approach, since there is a high level of dependence on the skills and resources of the contractor in any case. Equally, where there is interdependence between the owner and a contractor due to special technology, similar considerations apply.

2.4.5 Summary

To recap, the following factors make projects especially suitable for the alliancing approach described in this book:

- the owner wants to achieve better than historical cost and/or schedule performance
- the project represents a significant capital investment
- the project is technically or organisationally complex
- the project involves high levels of uncertainty
- there are (relatively) few suppliers able to deliver the specific service required.

The reality is that in major projects today many of the above factors are likely to be present, and it is essential for an owner to be able to deliver a complex, high-quality installation not only in record time but also at a lower cost than has been achieved previously. The discussion is no longer about either a low cost or a fast schedule, but is one of a low cost and a fast schedule.

3. Potential barriers to alliancing

Summary

Potential barriers that can inhibit adopting an alliancing approach are identified and discussed in this section under five main headings.

With the exception of owner skills, most of these barriers can be viewed as being primarily self-imposed and resulting from the way in which organisations are structured and the ways in which they have been used to conducting their business.

Initiation of change normally results from dissatisfaction with the *status quo*. For change to be effective this dissatisfaction needs to recognised by organisational leaders, brought to the fore and actions taken to achieve the changes that are required. It is also acknowledged that human nature is such that in-built resistance to change will exist in most organisations, so specific attention needs to be paid to encouraging and supporting changes in the cultural attitudes of individuals.

Contents

- **Organisational structures**
  Hierarchical organisations
  Matrix organisations

- **Cultural attitudes**
  Little low-level empowerment
  Little peer group contact
  Blaming not sharing
  Reluctance to communicate freely
  Lack of real commitment
  Ingrained distrust
  Investment in inappropriate skills
  Avoidance of personal accountability
  Rigid roles and procedures

- **Partner fit**

- **Commercial concerns**

- **Owner skills**

For an organisation to move to alliancing, the issues are likely to be the same or similar as in any other change initiative. Typically, very few organisations change unless there is sufficient dissatisfaction with the current situation and this is highlighted by the leaders of the organisation. However, even when the need for change is quite clear and has been recognised by the leaders of the organisation, effecting the necessary changes can still be difficult. A principal reason for this is that the majority of individuals are inherently resistant to change. For most individuals it is more comfortable to deal with the *status quo*, however imperfect, rather than face the challenges and opportunities that come with change.

The response when faced with the possibility of having to change is often one of seeking to 'prove' that the proposed changes will either not work, will be too risky for the organisation or cannot be made because of some externally imposed restraint. There are, of course, other potential barriers to change which are more tangible.

The principal purpose of this section is to highlight areas and issues that should be considered in making a decision to move to alliancing. Four areas that are of specific interest in relation to alliancing are covered:

- organisational structures
- cultural attitudes
- commercial concerns
- availability of owner skills.

Where considered appropriate, approaches to surmounting potential barriers are offered, as are observations on how some of the specific features of alliancing can play a part in this.

3.1 Organisational structures

3.1.1 Hierarchical organisations

Many organisations have adopted the structure of a military hierarchy with many tiers of command, each level of management being responsible for a small number of subordinates. This model evolved largely as a result of communication restraints and also to promote efficiency.

Issues around complex work processes were solved by the creation of many specialist tasks, each handled by a different group of people. While this has provided a strong direction and a good flow of information in situations of stability, the organisational form is not good at coping with the dynamic environment necessary to realise a project. Hierarchies are predisposed to prevent cross-flows of communication, thus sacrificing speed and flexibility. Furthermore, suboptimisation is introduced into work processes, with each department or group of individuals optimising their own piece of the work without looking at the impact on the total result.

Hierarchies promote a culture of moving responsibility and accountability upwards, and are not suited to the horizontal team-based working required for the realisation of major projects in the short time frames that the economic environment demands. Many owner organisations were designed traditionally to cope with the relatively steady-state problems of operating a productive facility. Contracting organisations have had to cope with much more flexibility and adaptability to new circumstances, since their workload, work volume and resource levels are unpredictable.

3.1.2 Matrix organisations

The development of the matrix organisation overcame many of the limitations of the pure hierarchy in organisations whose business is realising major projects. Matrix organisations work with task forces led by a project manager, who draws on resources supplied by departments organised as shown in Figure 5. The departments are responsible for supplying suitably skilled staff to the projects. However, once assigned to a project the staff are controlled by the project manager, who is the person accountable for the results of the project team.

Figure 5

The matrix organisation

In an alliance the aim is to form an overall task force organisation (the single integrated project team) which is led by the overall project manager. In an overall task force organisation the individual project managers from the different alliance partners take direct accountability for their scopes of work and participate in the project management team. Individuals from one organisation may also be working under the control of one of the project managers of another alliance partner.

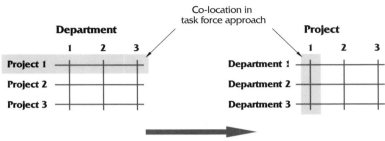

Move from strong departments to strong projects

Organisations that have retained a strong departmental influence in a matrix structure are likely to experience resistance from the departmental organisations, which are not used to devolving their power to project managers, let alone to an alliance in which project managers from other organisations are active participants in the management team.

3.2 Cultural attitudes

Organisations develop cultures over time that give common meaning to life in the workplace. These cultures define the pattern to which individual human behaviour conforms in a particular environment. Culture is conditioned by the environment within which relationships are conducted, and it is modified by the accumulated experience and the attitude of individuals. Therefore, in most organisations the existence of culture is felt most strongly when individuals exhibit behaviour that conflicts with the 'way things are done around here'.

Since, by definition, an alliance project will bring together companies with different cultures, specific actions will have to be taken to surmount cultural barriers. One way to achieve this is to work to create a project culture that is separate from the cultures of any one of the organisational cultures represented. Many alliances have found that creating a separate identity for the project that all team members can align behind is of particular value in starting this process.

Specific cultural characteristics that may be a barrier to effective alliancing are described below. For each, an approach to overcome the impact of the characteristic is offered should the symptoms be encountered. Ways in which specific features of alliancing can assist are also noted where appropriate.

3.2.1 Little low-level empowerment

In traditional hierarchies power has been restricted to the higher levels of organisations, and this has limited the speed of decision-making and promoted a culture of buck-passing. This means that there is little attempt at resolving problems at the level where they are first recognised.

Emphasising the importance of individual contributions is essential in the early days of the alliance. The use of the financial incentive scheme and the search for better ways of doing things reinforce each other. There is a direct reward to the project for innovation. Instituting a recognition and reward scheme for individual project members or groups of people will ensure that behaviour in support of the new approach is reinforced, and this will strengthen and accelerate the drive for change.

3.2.2 Little peer group contact

Due to the elevation of decision-making described above, there has been little value attached to working level relationships between different parties. Working methods have been primarily transaction based, defined by the contract in force. This has resulted in there being no incentive to deal with issues on a peer group contact basis. Thus the full resources of organisations are not mobilised effectively.

In conventional contracts, project managers of the main contractors and subcontractors generally meet only to resolve problems and discuss disputes, and not to plan the execution of the project together. The use of a single integrated project management team with responsibility for the total project, supported by an alliance board of senior executives whose companies have a direct financial stake, will help ensure that different ways of working are compared and the most suitable one for the job in hand is selected.

3.2.3 Blaming not sharing

Individuals have not been encouraged to concentrate on mutually owning and solving problems across organisational boundaries. The commercial environment has encouraged the automatic blaming of problems on others and the withholding of cooperation for fear of the assumption of legal responsibility. This has usually delayed solutions and made them more costly. It has been a major source of friction at working level.

The financial incentive scheme mechanism of alliancing removes the commercial pressure to leave the blame with someone else and keeps attention on solving the problem. Commercial risk is taken jointly by the owner and the alliance partners, and it is in everyone's interest that problems are solved for the lowest cost; it is of secondary interest which partner pays for it.

3.2.4 Reluctance to communicate freely

Individuals tend to feel that communicating freely will expose them to unwanted responsibility or personal risk. An atmosphere of 'no comment' develops when problems are discussed. Also, early knowledge of problems is withheld, either for fear of exposing 'failings' or, alternatively, in the hope that somehow the problem will be resolved without anyone else ever getting to know about it. This lack of free communication can foster an adversarial attitude.

The generation of an open project environment, where communication from the leadership is direct to all team members rather than cascaded through a hierarchy, will tend to unlock people's reluctance to communicate (individuals are not left to compare distorted and conflicting messages from the organisation's leadership). Furthermore, there is no benefit to allowing another member of the alliance to create a problem which subsequently becomes a joint problem.

3.2.5 Lack of real commitment

The traditional working environment has not encouraged a commitment to improvement. At the lower levels of organisations there is almost always a suspicion that management is not really committed to change and, as a consequence, the individual may be exposed to criticism and risk if he attempts to make improvements. At the upper levels of management there may also be a tendency to dismiss the possibility that individuals at lower levels have anything really worthwhile to contribute. This will be readily evident to those at the lower levels and will adversely impact on their level of commitment.

The personal commitment of project team members is vital to the success of an alliance project and is heavily dependent on the commitment of senior managers. The whole process of selecting alliance partners and the design of the alliance is aimed at generating commitment at the senior levels. There can only be joint success or failure, both at the individual and at the corporate level. The commercial alignment mechanism helps ensure that there is an incentive to encourage ideas for performance improvements from all levels. Senior managers within the alliance participants, as well as those assigned to the project, must also exhibit behaviours and attitudes that will be seen to be supportive of those at the lower levels.

3.2.6 Ingrained distrust

The traditional working environment has created an automatic distrust between owner and contractor staff of each other's motives. A view prevails that opposite numbers will take immediate advantage of any relaxation. This militates against cooperation in dealing with issues. This problem can only be addressed by the giving of trust to other parties in the belief that it will not be abused. For a successful alliance this has to be the approach because there is too little time to wait and see if the right to trust has been earned by a party's actions.

3.2.7 Investment in inappropriate skills

The traditional adversarial environment has promoted the development of special skills in dealing with issues on a contractual basis. Certain key members of both the owner's and the contractor's staff have built up an expertise they do not want to see devalued. Thus change is viewed as a threat to personal job security and is resisted.

The new way of working will require adjustment for some people. The policing role of the owner is removed, as is the overreliance on contractual relationships. In this case individuals will have to identify a new role for themselves or accept that this new approach is not for them.

3.2.8 Avoidance of personal accountability

The traditional ways of doing business provided a measure of collective security which could be disturbed by adopting change. There is a natural reluctance to be the first to stick one's head above the parapet. The emphasis of a no-blame culture in a partnership is necessary to change people's mind-set. Once this is recognised to be real and the leadership behaves accordingly, the tendency will be for individuals to take accountability beyond their normal remit and focus on the contribution they can make to the overall result.

3.2.9 Rigid roles and procedures

Traditional methods of working have encouraged the development of rigidly defined roles and a plethora of standard operating procedures. This has been a consequence of the hierarchical organisation. It reflects a military approach to dealing with issues. Procedures have been developed that seek to minimise or remove discretion at certain levels in organisations in the search for predictability. This was a response to the inadequate communication options available in the past, and prevents the adoption of the more effective options now available.

The permission to challenge procedures and concentrate on value streams is an important part of the search for improved performance. If people are being encouraged to innovate and yet have to adhere blindly to the owner's engineering specifications and procedures then the initiative will be short-lived. Likewise for roles, the alliance environment encourages individuals to define roles for themselves within the context of the project organisation that are consistent with achieving improved results. This is not an abdication of managerial responsibility, but a recognition that a purely top-down approach to defining responsibilities will inevitably be imperfect in the new situation and individuals need to be encouraged to fill in the cracks themselves. At the same time individuals should be released from non-value-adding activities that they identify.

3.3 Partner fit

Partner fit can be viewed in relation to the strategic and cultural fit of the partners. With regard to cultural fit, a concern that may be present relates to the perceived difficulties of creating a successful alliance with companies from different countries, and hence cultures. However, evidence suggests that, while it will almost certainly be necessary to take account of cultural diversity, it need not be a barrier. There are examples of very successful alliances composed of companies from, for example, Europe and Asia, North and South America and different countries in Europe.

Since survival in today's competitive environment requires companies to differentiate themselves as much as possible, the likelihood of two companies with identical cultures joining an alliance will be very unlikely. Cultural differences can be expected to be the norm rather than the exception. Willingness to understand cultural differences and to accept compromises in the face of cultural problems will be vital to the effectiveness of the alliance.

Strategic fit, on the other hand, is an issue that does need to be addressed, because fundamentally alliances are formed to give strategic advantage. Good strategic fit will always be an advantage for an alliance in that it will strengthen its purpose, while a lack of strategic fit is likely to have the opposite impact.

While companies may be culturally compatible, it is unlikely that this on its own will sufficiently compensate for a lack of strategic fit. Companies with a good strategic fit have the opportunity to adjust themselves to each other's cultures, even if these are significantly different, and will have an incentive to do so.

Strategic fit centres around the complementary nature of skills and assets and the business aspirations. Surveys have suggested that partner skills should not overlap. This view is consistent with academic literature, where alliance strength is often seen to derive from the co-specialisation of skills and resources. Competitive tension introduced by the inclusion of more than one party offering comparable skills or services has the possibility of destroying the creation of effective relationships. Having said that, however, there are examples of alliances that have been very successful even though they did include members who in normal circumstances would be direct competitors. This probably points to the fact that the companies concerned had a good strategic fit in terms of their business aspirations, and this was the dominant factor in determining how their relationship within the alliance developed.

3.4 Commercial concerns

The alliance model described in this book uses a financial incentive scheme as the commercial alignment mechanism, with a target cost usually being one of the principle criteria. At the same time it is based on selecting contractors before the project is fully defined. The usual and understandable initial reaction of an owner is that this leaves him commercially exposed:

■ How can I be sure that the deal put together is a good one?
■ How competitive is the target cost?
■ Is there not an obvious conflict of interest between the contracting parties and the owner?
■ How do I know that the target cost is not being set so high that the contractors will finish up with excessive profits?

These are all natural concerns of owners, but the fact is that contractors also have genuine concerns, and indeed may share some of those that the owner has. Concerns that contractors may have include:

■ How difficult will the targets be to achieve?
■ Will I be forced into accepting a target cost that I believe is too low and just not achievable?
■ Can I rely on the other contractors to be open and 'honest'?

A combination of processes can be used to provide the necessary assurance to all parties.

First, in the formative stages of the alliance, starting with the processes to select contractors, the owner should give a clear indication of what will have to be achieved (capital cost, project schedule, Internal Rate of Return (IRR) or any other appropriate criteria) in order for final approval for the project to proceed to be given. It will probably also be appropriate for the owner to make it clear that he does expect the contractors' 'normal' levels of profit to be included as part of the target capital cost. This will help provide reassurance to contractors that the owner is not seeking to achieve his aims by squeezing their profitability. Above all, it is vitally important that any figures put forward by the owner are genuine. Setting clear criteria to be achieved for project approval provides a very clear context for the work that is undertaken to develop and define the project and to establish the cost estimates and schedules from which the target criteria for the incentive scheme will be derived.

Second, the selection process for the contractors can require them to provide binding cost data which can be applied in building up cost estimates once the definition of the project has been developed.

Third, there are a number of processes that can be used to validate the cost estimate and schedules for, and hence the appropriateness of, any proposed targets derived from them. These include:

- bench-marking of the project cost by external experts
- extensive estimate reviews by owner and alliance partner representatives (i.e. independent of the project team)
- use of market data from the alliance partner bidding processes
- use of historical cost information for similar projects.

Finally, the owner will always have the ultimate veto in that he can decide that it would be inappropriate for him to proceed if the project approval criteria he set have not been met. Equally, each contractor will always have the right not to sign up to an incentive scheme that he believes is not in his interests.

Setting and agreeing appropriate targets is in the interests of all the parties, and so they should all be supportive of there being an intensive review period making use of the above checks and balances so that they can reach agreement. By using a rigorous review and challenge process the owner knows that the project is viable at the target cost and the contractors are presumably prepared to accept the challenge. All of this, of course, requires planning and effort.

3.5 Owner skills

Owners may be reluctant to embrace alliancing, either because they do not have project management skills within their own organisation or, even when they do, because they perceive there is a lack of people within their organisation that have been exposed to this approach and can therefore lead the development of an alliance model, from both the project management and the commercial viewpoints. However, these deficiencies can be overcome by supplementing the owner's organisation through the judicious use of consultants who have direct and relevant contract and project management experience of setting up alliance arrangements. The owner (and eventually the other members of the alliance) can also be supported by other consulting organisations that specialise in the facilitation of behavioural and cultural aspects of alliancing and in high performance team building. The 'independence' of such consultants is an important part of their ability to be effective, so if an owner decides to follow this route it is important that care is taken not to prejudice this 'independence'. For example, it is recommended that anyone so employed should not have a financial interest in the incentive scheme. As the concept becomes more widely practised and more knowledge is disseminated (such as through this book), the lack of owner skills should become less of an issue.

The two most important things from an owner's perspective are:

- A willingness to step out and try something new and confront the uncertainty that accompanies it. Anecdotal evidence from successful alliances confirms that the approach is supported by people rather readily because intuitively it makes sense.
- Identifying personnel with the leadership skills which are required during the formation of an alliance and throughout the execution of the project. People with good interpersonal skills are required to make the alliance work. Problems have to be resolved through consensus-based decision-making with the one goal of choosing the solution that is best for the project. This contrasts with the skills required in resolving traditional problems, which have been based on adversarial contractual posturing and leverage.

4. Legal considerations

Summary

This section examines the key pieces of European legislation that can impact on the competitive selection of contractors and the formation of cooperative ventures such as alliances as described in this book. It considers the legislation in the context of all forms of partnering.

Insofar as European Union legislation is concerned, there are no specific impediments to the alliancing approach as described in this book. Indeed, with regard to competitive selection of contractors in particular, it is clear that companies can be selected on best economic value criteria and that this does not limit the selection consideration only to bid price.

However, there are a number of legal issues that need to be considered by the parties as they enter into any form of partnering agreement, especially if the agreement is not one of an *ad hoc* or project-specific nature, and these are highlighted for review.

Contents

- Competition and fair trading
- Public sector procurement directives
- Proposals for change in the public sector
- Utilities Directive
- Concessions and other forms of public–private partnership
- Employment issues
  European Union Acquired Rights Directive (ARD)
  – Application of the ARD to partnering arrangements
  – Effects of the ARD
  – Considerations for partnering and alliancing contracts
  – Non-application of the ARD
  The use of integrated teams

Many people who are new to the concept of alliancing are initially concerned that implementing it will contravene legislative provisions. In broad terms this is not so and, insofar as the European Union is concerned, there are no specific legal impediments to alliancing. There are, however, a number of legal issues that need to be fully taken into account from the start of the process to put an alliance in place. The most important of these are discussed in this section.

4.1 Competition and fair trading

Laws and regulations both at the European Union and, in many countries, at national level prohibit agreements that prevent, restrict or distort competition (subject to the power of the European Commission to grant exemptions), or which amount to abuse of a dominant position in the relevant market. For example, anticompetitive effects can result variously from long-term exclusive partnering or alliance agreements (note that exclusivity can arise from the effect of the agreement of satisfying the employer's total requirements for the relevant goods or services, as well as from an express exclusivity obligation). Abusive behaviour results when, for example, a dominant contractor extracts oppressive or discriminatory terms, when the owner is tied into taking goods or services unrelated to those which are the subject matter of the contract or where the contract prices are predatory (i.e. below cost). The analysis will be a question of fact in each case.

The European Union prohibitions apply only if the anticompetitive aspects of the agreement appreciably affect actual or potential trade between European Union member states. An effect on interstate trade can be found even though the parties to the agreement reside in the same member state and the agreement is to be performed in a single member state.

Local laws may apply to anticompetitive agreements that do not affect interstate trade. There are also specific restrictions (under the Utilities Directive 93/38 as amended by Directive 98/4/EC) on the use by utilities of framework agreements which 'hinder, limit or distort' competition. These restrictions too may apply even where there is no effect on interstate trade.

(A partnering or alliance agreement which includes a transfer of business assets may also give rise to one or more 'mergers' for the purposes of European Union and national competition laws. If, in such circumstances, certain other jurisdictional thresholds are met, the parties may be legally obliged to obtain merger clearance from the relevant competition authorities before implementing the agreement. The legal and jurisdictional rules differ around the European Union, and need to be checked in each case.)

Most partnering or alliancing agreements are unlikely to give rise to competition or fair trading issues. Where they do, it may be possible to avoid any impact by reducing the scope or term of the agreement, or, where this is not considered desirable, by seeking appropriate assurances or exemptions from the European Commission or the relevant national authorities.

4.2 Public sector procurement directives

The public sector procurement directives (The Supply Directive 93/36, the Works Directive 93/37, the Services Directive 92/50 and the Remedies Directive 89/665 as amended by Directive 97/52/EC), while requiring competition to be transparent and open to contractors from all member states, include a number of elements which assist partnering.

As an alternative to lowest price, contract award can be made according to 'the most economically advantageous offer', provided that the criteria for this are clearly stated prior to tendering. These can include criteria relating to partnering such as:

- understanding and experience of partnering or alliancing
- organisation structure proposed to effect partnering or alliancing, and/or
- methods proposed to spread partnering or alliancing throughout the organisation

where the purchaser considers such factors would be to its economic advantage.

Award procedures for public works which are above the threshold of the public sector procurement directives will be:

- *Open*, where all interested parties must be allowed to tender.
- *Restricted*, where only selected persons may tender.
- *Negotiated*. In the public sector at present the negotiated procedure can only be used under the very limited circumstances provided for in the directives. It is discussed further, in the context of the Utilities Directive (see Section 4.4, below).

The open and restricted award procedures for public works are illustrated schematically in Figures 6 and 7 and the essential difference between the two is highlighted. Public authorities have a free choice of which procedure to adopt, but authorities wishing to partner generally follow the restricted route. The open procedure suffers from the disadvantages of allowing unlimited numbers to be invited to tender.

4.3 Proposals for change in the public sector

The European Commission has put forward proposals to amend the public sector procurement directives in order to allow:

- A specific right to use framework contracts. These are contracts for a specified period with several contractors by which the public authority holds a competition between the contractors signed up to the framework contract for the award of individual contracts under it from time to time.
- Competitive dialogue. This would replace the existing negotiated procedure with prior publication of a notice and is expected to be more widely available than the existing negotiated procedure. At the least, it is expected to be available for long-term projects similar to UK Private Finance Initiative projects or in cases where the public authority cannot establish specifications on its own.

Such amendments, if implemented, will further assist partnering by allowing public authorities to tender contracts between a small group of contractors with whom they have a longer term relationship, and by permitting discussions on

Figure 6

The open award procedure

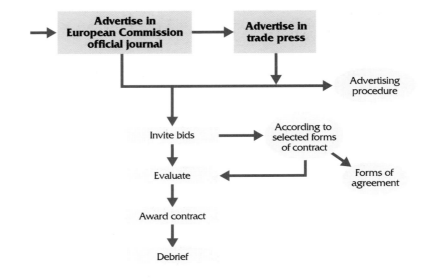

Figure 7

The restricted award procedure

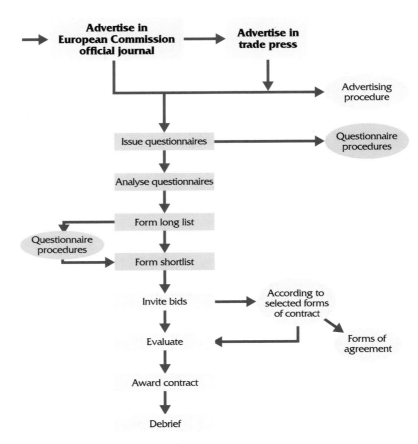

specifications and, probably, pricing during the award procedure, in order to align the parties' incentives and objectives.

4.4 Utilities Directive

The utilities sector has a more flexible procurement regime. In addition to the open and restricted procedures, which are substantially the same as in the public sector, there is an unrestricted right to use the negotiated procedure (see Figure 8), which is particularly suited to partnering and alliancing.

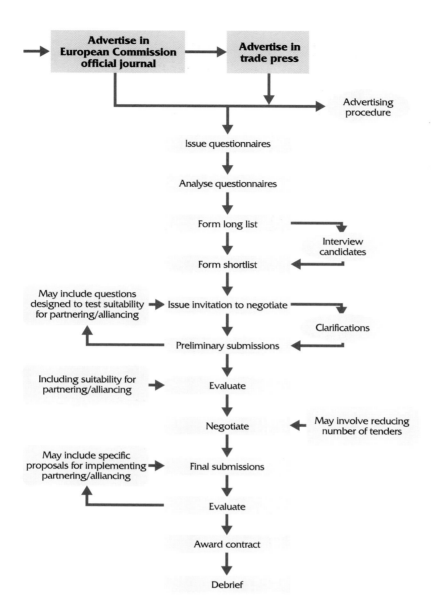

Figure 8

The negotiated award procedure

There is also an express right to use framework agreements. These can be agreements with several contractors, permitting competition within a small group, similar to the proposed public sector framework contracts described above. Alternatively, subject to competition and fair trading considerations, a utility may enter into a framework agreement permitting a single contractor to carry out a series of projects over a period of time. The use of such framework agreements is particularly suited to longer term partnering.

4.5 Concessions and other forms of public–private partnership

In general, the public sector procurement directives do not regulate concessions and other forms of public–private partnership. However, there are limited requirements for works concessions, including a requirement to advertise in the European

Commission's official journal. The European Commission has indicated that, in its view, the underlying treaty obligations apply to such relationships as well as to the award of contracts, and would generally mean that the private sector concessionaire or partner should be selected through some form of competitive procedure. Where partnering or alliancing is contemplated, a procedure involving negotiation is likely to be preferred.

4.6 Employment issues

Although most partnering and alliancing arrangements are unlikely to have consequences for the employees of the parties concerned, it is important to consider whether there may be any consequences and, if so, what they are. The relevant aspects of European Union legislation and practical considerations that arise in relation to partnering contracts are discussed below.

4.6.1 European Union's Acquired Rights Directive

The European Union's Acquired Rights Directive (ARD) (EU Council Directive 77/187, 14 February 1977, as amended by Council Directive 98/50, 29 June 1998) was introduced to safeguard employees' rights in the event of transfers of undertakings, businesses or parts of businesses. The consequences of its application are summarised below. The ARD has been implemented through domestic legislation in European Union member states and, accordingly, regard must be had to the implementing legislation in the relevant European jurisdiction in which the partnering arrangement takes place. Revised implementing legislation complying with amendments to the ARD adopted in June 1998 must be brought into force by 17 July 2001.

Application of the ARD to partnering arrangements
The parties must consider whether the ARD will apply to the partnering arrangement. This will be the case if there is a *transfer* of an *undertaking* from one party to another (or into a new jointly controlled entity) at any stage in the partnering process, for example:

- on the award of a contract
- on a change of contractor, or
- at the end of the contract.

The term *undertaking* has been broadly defined in case law (*Ayse Süzen v Zehnacker Gebäudereinigung GmbH Krankenhausservice*, Case C-13/95 [1997] 1 CMLR 768). The European Court of Justice decided that an undertaking is an economic entity comprising an identifiable function, with its own workforce and assets and a certain degree of organisational autonomy. Such an entity must have a degree of stability. For example, an arrangement where work is carried out on an *ad hoc* basis will not normally be an economic entity, nor will the completion of outstanding work under a specific single project (*Rygaard* v *Stro Molle Akustik A/S*, Case C-48/94 [1996] 3 CMLR 45). However, contracted-out services may comprise an undertaking.

In assessing whether there is a *transfer* of an undertaking, the European Court of Justice has decided (*Spijkers* v *Gebroeders Benedik Abbatoir*, CV: 24/85 [1986] 2 CMLR 296) that the factors to be considered include whether assets, either tangible or intangible, are transferred, and whether employees are taken over.

Where, on the award of a contract, there is, in addition to the assignment of an identifiable function (i.e. the role in the relevant construction project), a transfer of assets, such as land or equipment, or of some staff, it is likely that the ARD will apply.

The circumstances in which the ARD will apply on a change in contractor are, as a result of the Suzen case, more limited. It will only apply if there is a transfer either of significant tangible or intangible assets to the new contractor, or the taking over of a major part of the workforce in terms of their numbers or skills by the new contractor.

Whether the ARD will apply at the end of the contract will depend on the same factors as apply on the award of a contract. However, in the case of long contracts it is possible that the test for the applicability of the ARD may change before the end of the contract.

In any event, the parties should take legal advice on the likely application of the ARD to the partnering arrangement and, in the interests of certainty, agree whether the ARD is to apply to the arrangement.

Effects of the ARD

The possible effects of the application of the ARD to a partnering arrangement are the following:

- the employees of the owner assigned to the project to which the arrangement relates may automatically become employed by the contractor or the new jointly controlled entity upon the commencement of provision of services by the contractor (unless they elect not to transfer but to resign instead);
- the contractor or the new entity is required to employ the employees on the same terms and conditions, excluding terms and conditions relating to an occupational pension;
- the employees' continuity of employment is preserved;
- dismissals in connection with the transfer will be unfair unless they are for an 'economic, technical or organisational reason entailing changes in the workforce';

■ the owner and the contractor or new entity must inform and consult employee representatives; and

■ the contractor or new entity will assume employment liabilities of the owner in relation to the employees.

On the application of the ARD at the end of a contract, any employees employed by the contractor or new entity in relation to the project (including employees appointed by the contractor or new entity who were not originally employees of the owner) may become employed by the owner, and the same effects described above, but vice versa, will apply.

Considerations for partnering or alliancing contracts

The parties should consider the following issues and, where necessary, agree appropriate provisions for inclusion in the partnering contract:

■ identity of transferring employees
■ numbers of transferring employees
  – possibility of redundancies
  – evaluation of the tender in the light of potential redundancy costs
  – apportionment of redundancy costs
■ terms and conditions of employment applicable to transferring employees
■ control conferred on the contractor or third party over employees
  – ability to change terms and conditions during contract
  – ability to appoint new employees
  – ability to direct employees
■ provision of information by the contractor or third party on employee numbers, dismissal of employees and changes to terms and conditions
■ termination of contract
  – redeployment of employees
  – apportionment of any redundancy costs.

Non-application of the ARD

Where it is considered that the ARD will not apply, it may nevertheless be the case that, for the success of the project, the contractor or third party will require the transfer of key employees. This can be achieved by the owner seconding those employees to the contractor or the new jointly controlled entity, or terminating the employment of the employees by notice and offers being made for new employment to take effect from the termination date on similar terms and conditions of employment. The arrangements for this may be dealt with in the partnering or the alliancing contract.

4.6.2 The use of integrated teams

A number of European Union member states have legislation (e.g. the Belgian law dated 24 July 1987 concerning temporary staff) which prohibits or places restrictions on arrangements that have the effect of placing employees at the disposal of another employer. Care should be taken to avoid breaching the requirements of such legislation when placing employees in integrated teams.

Part 2

Implementing an alliance – a tool-kit

1. Introduction

The purpose of this part of the book is to provide a practical guide to implementing the main steps in setting up an alliance. It starts from the premise that the owner organisation has taken the decision to pursue an alliancing approach and has committed itself to driving the process through its business and project organisations. The tool-kit is split into sections, each of which deals with a specific aspect of alliancing. As a consequence, material which is relevant to each of the main steps may be located in various places in the book. The main steps in implementing an alliance are illustrated in Figure 9. This also provides an outline of the key activities and processes for each of the steps and a guide to where material related to them can be found in this book.

The tool-kit draws its examples and recommendations from a number of successful alliance projects that contributors to this document have experienced, even though the specific projects are not identified. Examples from less successful alliances are used principally to demonstrate that failure to deliver the benefits expected can often be traced to an inadequate understanding and application of the basic principles highlighted in this book.

A word of caution is that the success of an alliance form cannot be guaranteed by a step-wise application of a linear recipe. Once initiated, many of the activities and processes within each of the main steps will overlap with activities and processes associated with subsequent steps. It is also emphasised that the processes described here are tools to assist and guide companies that have a desire to achieve exceptional results through 'breaking the mould' of the traditional contracting process. In view of this it is recommended that those using the tool-kit should not hesitate to adapt the processes and procedures as may be considered appropriate to meet their own specific circumstances. In making adaptations, however, care must be exercised to ensure that the fundamental principles are retained.

Finally, it is emphasised that the emotional human side of commitment needs to be present in the leaders that are embarking on an alliance venture, in addition to the rational, contractual and deterministic approach to expectations that is traditionally the norm.

Figure 9 (opposite)
The alliance implementation process: a brief guide

Alliance development stage	Key activities and issues	Location of relevant material		
		Part 1	**Part 2**	**Appendices**
Owner decision to alliance	Understanding alliancing concept and requirements	Sections 1–4	5.1–5.3	
	Suitable circumstances	2.4		
	Business needs/drivers	2.4		
	Evaluation of alternative strategies	2.4		
	Senior management alignment and commitment	1.3.3	2.1	
Owner preparatory steps	Internal alignment: • identify champions/project leaders • business team/project team alignment • owner competencies and role • owner team		Section 2 2.1 2.2 2.2.1 2.2.2	
	Establish alliance contracting/formation strategy: • alliance design • timing of selection • contract structures • remuneration terms • selection process (open, restricted, negotiated)	4.2–4.5	4.1 4.2 4.3 Section 5, 5.1 5.4.2 4.4	
	Alliance contractor selection process: • establish selection criteria • prepare selection (tender) documentation • prepare selection evaluation plan		Section 4, 4.4 4.5 4.5 4.6	
Alliance partner selection	Owner communication of intent to potential alliance contractors		Section 3	
	Issue selection (tender) documents			
	Evaluate responses and select		4.5, 4.6	
Alliance development, alignment and commitment	Build alliance relationships: • apply facilitation, training, coaching and team building • develop and apply communication processes • apply/design other alignment mechanisms • develop and institute performance improvement and innovation processes	1.3.8	Section 9 9.3 7.2 9.2 9.4	
	Jointly develop: • project technical definition • execution plans and programmes (schedules) • cost estimates • risk analyses		6.2.2 6.2.1 6.2.1	Appendix 2
	Finalise works contracts for execution phase		5.1–5.4	
	Develop and finalise alliance agreement: • project objectives • principles of relationship • project performance measures • incentive scheme • roles, responsibilities and decision-making • dispute resolution		5.1, 5.2, 5.5, Section 6 5.5.1 5.5.2 5.5.3, 6.2, 6.4 5.5.3, Section 6 5.5.2 5.5.2	Appendices 2 & 3 Appendix 1
	Design and establish integrated project organisation	1.3.5	7.1	
	Identify/develop common processes and procedures		Section 8	
	Build relationships with other parties: • non-alliance companies • external authorities • miscellaneous		Section 11 11.1 11.2 11.3	

Owner's final approval to proceed with project

Alliance development stage	Key activities and issues	Part 1	Part 2	Appendices
Develop and sustain alliance	Establish team delivery targets			Appendix 2
	Monitor and modify project organisation, as appropriate		7.1.1	
	Monitor relationship quality		10.3	
	Continue: • performance improvement and innovation processes • facilitation, training, coaching and team building • building and sustaining relationships with others		9.4 9.3 Section 11	
	Monitor and report performance against incentive scheme targets		10.1	

Project development and definition phase (informal alliance)

Project execution phase (formal alliance)

2. The owner internal alignment process

Summary

This section covers the importance of alignment within the owner's organisation and the specific importance of commitment to the concept at the highest levels of the owner's organisation if alliancing is to be successfully implemented.

It then covers the need for the owner's business and project management personnel to be aligned in regard to the specific project, and particularly in respect of the business objectives and performance requirements for that project.

The role of the owner's team is then discussed. Here the emphasis is on developing clarity about the role and taking account of the owner's competencies.

Finally, the composition of the owner's project team is discussed.

Contents

- The importance of owner alignment

- Owner commitment

- Business and project alignment

- Owner role and competencies

- The owner's project team

Alignment within the owner's organisation is an essential prerequisite of creating a successful alliance, as it is out of alignment that true commitment is generated. This alignment is probably best considered in two contexts:

- general alignment within and across the organisation
- alignment related to a specific project.

The importance of alignment lies in two main areas. First, the owner as the initiating party has a particular burden of responsibility to establish sufficiently broad support for the new approach in his own organisation before engaging members of the contracting and supply community, whom he will want to be persuaded of the benefits of adopting what, for many, will be an entirely new way of working, and have them be willing to enter into an alliance arrangement. Success in persuading others willingly to adopt an alliance approach, and the ultimate success of the alliance itself, will depend as much as anything else on the owner's personnel (particularly those at senior levels) being seen to speak and act in concert with the philosophy. Where demonstrated behaviours are seen to deviate from the stated philosophy there can be little expectation that the necessary commitment and alignment can be generated in the other organisations that will largely influence the project outcome.

Second, for many organisations the effectiveness of the owner's project team, and thus of the project as a whole, will depend on receiving support from various departments within the owner's organisation. If these supporting departments are not aligned to the alliancing approach, their involvement has a significant potential to frustrate the aims and objectives of the alliance.

Introducing a fundamental change in contracting strategy is analogous to any other major change initiative insofar as the organisational repercussions are concerned. Some of the barriers to change of this nature are discussed in Part 1 of this book.

Examples of two areas in which such changes may be required are given below.

Example 1. The adoption of an alliancing approach will impact on the traditional procurement function in many organisations, and is likely to lessen the impact and power of the procurement group. If such traditional attitudes prevail, the loss of formal power makes the procurement group a source of potential resistance. For years these organisations have been given the role of protecting corporate funds, through price-based selections that have often focused on price today rather than, say, the total installed or life-cycle results of the future.

Example 2. Owner engineers who have had the traditional role of checking the efforts of the design contractor are going to have to re-evaluate their role to one of support of and assistance to the contractor who will be accountable for the design in an alliance. The role of the owner specialist is to ensure that the functional requirements of the facility will be met by the designs proposed. This is a positive, generative role, as opposed to a reactive 'send it back and let them get it right' approach.

The types of transformations in role and approach identified in the examples above will not come easily to many people. Also, as the new future becomes clearer, points of open and covert resistance are likely to emerge within the organisation. In common with other change initiatives, the resistance likely to be encountered will revolve around the perceived winners and losers.

In the course of the alignment generating process and achieving the changes that are required, constant communication of the purpose, goals and philosophy of the new approach is essential. This is the task of the senior corporate management, who must continually reinforce the message that this is the future way for the organisation on the one hand, and of the project leadership on the other, who must lead by example.

2.1 Owner commitment

While the very highest levels of management (i.e. board level) will generally be receptive to any initiative that holds the promise of improving business performance, it is nonetheless vital that they are fully committed to its implementation and prepared to give it the support that it requires. However, achieving the promised benefits is the task of senior managers. It is the commitment demonstrated by these senior managers that will determine the success of the subsequent implementation steps. To inspire those that are looking for a better way will be easy compared to convincing the traditionalists whose very expertise gives them a direct interest in the continuation of the traditional, well-tried approaches.

Some owner organisations have found it useful to appoint a champion to drive the communication and alignment process. For others, the enthusiasm and commitment of one or more key individuals who were leaders in the business and project teams demonstrating the value of the approach through successful application on a specific project has been key, with such success then providing a basis for generating enthusiasm, alignment and commitment through the wider organisation. Yet others have found that a combination of these two approaches has been appropriate, and in many instances owners have reported that utilising external expert consultants has been of significant worth.

2.2 Business and project alignment

When it comes to a specific project, alignment within the owner organisation between the business management and the project team is essential. Without it the design of performance targets within a true business context will be absent, and these targets may then turn out to be artificial and contradictory. The premise for the risk and reward schemes that are presented later is that they are based on real business needs, and so the involvement of the accountable business management in setting and 'owning' authentic targets which meet the business needs of the owner is crucial. If an owner sets targets for contractors that require exceptional performance from others just as a contingency creating device, then the project contracting strategy will, and will be seen to, remain in the traditional risk-transferring rather than the risk-sharing domain.

2.2.1 Owner role and competencies

An integral part of the owner alignment process is to encourage an active debate about what the role of the owner will be for the purposes of realising the project.

This is important in that experience indicates that many owners' teams do not have real and specific understanding about their role. It is also consistent with a key principle of alliancing – that each party should have clearly defined accountabilities within a single integrated project team and avoiding duplication of effort.

The role of the owner's team will be directly related to the competencies he both possesses and wishes to deploy on the project. The owner must therefore also encourage an open and frank review of internal competencies and be willing to acknowledge where competencies are either weak or do not exist, and tailor the role of his team accordingly.

In some instances, the owner accountability may be limited simply to acquiring governmental permits, providing access to the site and supporting the contractor effort. In other cases, when the owner can bring specific expertise and value to the execution of a project, this should be recognised, and his accountabilities may be much more extensive.

Clarity of the role and accountabilities of the owner team should be addressed and taken into account in the design of the alliance structure to be formed. A thorough examination of existing competencies within an owner's organisation in the context of alliancing may also be useful in highlighting areas of deficiency that it would be valuable to enhance, as well as in highlighting competencies that are no longer relevant.

2.2.2 The owner team

Many contractor participants in an alliance, and even in some cases many of the owner's team, will only have a direct involvement during the construction phase of a capital project. The resulting facility will generate revenues for many years to come. Since the long-term life-cycle costs of an asset are becoming the subject of increasing focus, there is a natural concern within the owner's future asset management organisation that focus on capital cost alone could be at the expense of long-term operating cost. To reassure the asset management organisation and to ensure the overall success of the project, it is essential that the owner include operations and maintenance personnel in the project team from the earliest stages of the design. Their specific expertise and knowledge can provide valuable input to the design and construction process. These personnel can also help provide the balance that needs to be achieved between a low capital cost and fast construction schedule and a facility that is economical to operate.

3. Starting the process with potential alliance contractors

Summary

The success of an alliance is dependent on creating genuine alignment between all the participants. This section highlights the fact that genuine alignment cannot be gained merely by the owner imposing his will on the other participants.

The need for the owner to develop a clear strategy and plan for creating the intended alliance before engaging with potential alliance members and to communicate his intentions from the earliest contacts is also emphasised. Advice is given on some of the main points that need to be communicated.

The owner must be searching to create alignment from the start, and this requires him to conduct and require that others conduct all exchanges openly, while maintaining ethical integrity.

How and when the process of starting communications with potential alliance members will occur depends on a number of factors, but primarily on whether or not there is familiarity with the alliancing approach.

Contents

- Communicating the owner's intent
- Owner–contractor alignment

The success of an alliance depends on gaining the alignment and commitment of its member companies and of the individuals assigned to the project by the participating organisations. Selecting a weak or uncommitted member company can affect the performance of the entire project. True alignment and commitment of organisations is unlikely to be generated through a blind imposition of the approach by the owner. The genuine willingness of the selected contractors to work in this way is extremely important.

In many ways, the relationships between alliance partners is analogous to the marriage of two human beings, and it will only be a success if it is strongly desired, committed to and followed through enthusiastically by the parties. Without continuing desire, commitment and enthusiasm, marriage seldom works. The same applies to alliancing as a contracting strategy.

There is a fine distinction between imposing alliancing on contractors and offering them the opportunity to work with the owner with the ultimate intention of creating an alliance which is acceptable to all its members. Nevertheless, if the owner is truly committed to this approach and is genuine in his concern to seek solutions that meet both his and the contractors' needs, then the probability of success will be considerably enhanced.

The prudent owner will develop a coherent strategy and plan for introducing the concept to contractors who are potential alliance partners, and deal with the concerns, queries and issues that will almost certainly arise. This strategy should be tailored to individual circumstances. For example, if the concept is entirely new to the potential contractors, it may be appropriate for the owner to initiate dialogues with individual contractors, or seminars or workshops with groups of contractors, in advance of a formal selection process. These meetings would be aimed at introducing the contractors to and developing their understanding of the concept, thus enabling the contractors to be better prepared to deal with the details of the selection process.

3.1 Communicating the owner's intent

From the outset the owner must communicate clearly to potential alliance partners:

- his desire to adopt an alliancing approach, including very specifically a financial incentive scheme
- what he wants to get out of this approach
- why he considers the approach is likely to be beneficial to the alliance contractor members
- the criteria he is intending to apply in selecting contractors.

Among other things, this means that the owner must have developed a clear idea of what the key project drivers are (e.g. cost; schedule; performance guarantee; health, safety and environmental performance; operating cost; or a combination of some or all of these). More importantly, he must be willing to share these with the potential alliance partners. It is almost always of value if the project drivers are presented in the context of meeting the owner's overall business objectives.

There are also a number of other points which the owner needs to communicate to the potential alliance partners at the earliest appropriate opportunity. These include:

- *The contract structure that is envisaged.* The owner should also at the very least articulate the key concepts and basic general principles that he envisages will be applied in developing contracts, especially in respect of the alliance agreement.

- *The specific economic criteria or other measures that will have to be attained in order for final project approval to be forthcoming.* It is recognised that many owners have various projects competing for capital resources at any one time. As a result they may not be able to guarantee that final approval will be given, even if the criteria are met. If this does apply, the owner should make that clear to the contractors.

- *That the owner intends that the contractors selected will be involved in the execution phase, provided that approval to proceed is made, and subject always to their performance.* Without this sort of assurance, contractors will always be concerned that they are going to have to compete again to win the execution-phase contract. A likely consequence is that a contractor will be concerned to protect his competitive position, and may therefore be unwilling or less willing to bring forward all the ideas he has for optimising the project.

- *The need to agree at an early stage the ground rules, procedures, processes and methodologies for developing the definition of the project and, more specifically, the project cost estimates and implementation schedules.* Joint development cost estimates and implementation schedules is a key ingredient in building a solid foundation for an alliance. With cost estimates in particular, there is often a great deal of sensitivity and concern about revealing costs to other contractors, who may be regarded as competitors. Joint agreement on ground rules, etc., is an effective way of surmounting such problems.

- *The scope of any validation checks that will be applied to the jointly developed cost estimates and schedules, and procedures for resolving any issues that arise from them.* Many owners have well-established procedures for independent validation of cost estimates and schedules produced by project teams. If the contractors are unaware of these then difficulties and tensions can result when the validations are undertaken, particularly if the validation team considers that there are deficiencies in what the project team has produced.

3.2 Owner–contractor alignment

Alignment on agreed objectives between the owner and the contractor members of the alliance is crucial. As has been noted earlier, the formal mechanism and expression of alignment will be via the financial incentive scheme. Nevertheless, the owner also needs to ensure that he takes measures that will ensure he gains a full understanding of what the potential alliance partners are seeking to get out of participation in the project and what their drivers are (e.g. profit, revenue, a reference, technological development), as this will be an important factor in creating alignment.

A carefully structured questionnaire followed by a face-to-face debate can be an effective means of surfacing these points, but other mechanisms and approaches are possible. Whatever route is chosen, the key is that all exchanges are conducted openly, honestly and frankly and with integrity. Support at all levels in all the organisations involved is also important. If objectives cannot be aligned, there is no point in continuing. It becomes an arranged marriage or a marriage of convenience, which will be very unlikely to last.

4. Selecting alliance contractors

Summary

This section covers the crucial activity process of designing an alliance and selecting the right companies who will be its members.

The owner must develop a strategy for forming the alliance at an early stage, and advice on what should be covered in the strategy is provided.

Observations on factors that should be considered when deciding who should be members of the alliance are made and illustrated with examples.

This is then followed by advice on the timing of selection. The key point made is that selection should be made as early as possible.

A tried and tested general selection process is presented and discussed, as are some recommendations and examples of specific processes that have been used by successful alliancing practitioners.

This is followed by the identification and discussion of selection criteria that are considered to be appropriate when choosing alliance members.

Finally, advice is provided on the content and the benefits of having a detailed plan and process for evaluating the responses of competing contractors.

Contents

- Strategy
- Alliance design: number and type of members
- Timing of selection
- Selection process
- Selection criteria
- Evaluation plan and process

This section covers both the design or structure of the alliance to be formed and the process through which prospective alliance partners can be engaged. The purpose of the alliance design and alliance partner selection is to ensure that the right combination of contractors is invited to join the alliance and that the contractors selected are the best ones to realise the project goals of the owner.

4.1 Strategy

The owner should develop at an early stage an alliance formation strategy. This strategy should obviously take account of the specific nature and circumstances of the project as well as the needs and expectations of the owner. It should cover, among other things:

- the relevant areas of skills and expertise required to implement the project (e.g. process design, civil design, civil construction, mechanical erection and installation, electrical installation)
- the proposed composition of the alliance
- the proposed selection criteria
- the timing of selection
- the procedure and processes for selecting members of the alliance.

Subsequently, the tender documents should articulate:

- the alliance strategy proposed by the owner
- the needs of the project
- the expectations of the owner
- the intention to form an alliance
- the basic principles of the way of working together.

These factors, together with what is required of the bidders, should be explained in simple and relevant terms. The owner has a duty – and it is in his interest – to be clear about all these points and to make alliancing a central theme of the tender documents, rather than deal with them via a 'bolt-on' in an 'intent to alliance' paragraph.

4.2 Alliance design: the number and type of partners

The overall aim of the design of the alliance is to determine which grouping of contractors along with the owner is most likely to have the greatest influence on the project outcome. Having a clear understanding of the relevant areas of the skills and expertise that are required provides a basis for the owner to begin identifying the potential range of companies that might be included in the alliance. The range should then be fine tuned by the owner addressing critical questions, including:

- Can this party significantly influence the outcome of the project?
- Will the inclusion of this party in the alliance stimulate innovation to the benefit of the project?
- Will the inclusion of this party enable complexity to be managed better?

The number of members in an alliance will be highly dependent on the specific project, but one or two points are worth noting. It is unlikely to be either practical or appropriate to bring all the major supply-chain members into the main alliance. This would unduly increase the complexity of managing the project by the owner and the alliance members. On the other hand, restricting the number of members should not be regarded as a prime aim. There are examples of very successful alliances with as many as 12 to 15 members.

It should also be borne in mind that parties not included in the alliance can still be contracted in a way that is complementary to and supports the alliance approach. Use of alliance principles in the dealings with non-alliance suppliers and contractors will contribute to the overall success of the project (see Part 2, Section 11).

The parties that provoke an immediate 'yes' answer to the three questions above will often be those with high contract values which collectively represent a large percentage of the project budget. Care should be exercised to ensure that a focus on contract value does not lead to the exclusion of a contractor or supplier who could be particularly influential, as there can be unique high value-adding operations that can have a large influence on the success or failure of a project without them necessarily being the highest value contracts. Two examples are given below.

Example 1. An on-shore refinery restructuring project included the design, civil, mechanical and electrical and instrumentation contractors in the alliance without any major equipment suppliers. There were many pieces of major equipment from different suppliers. However, no one supplier was considered critical enough to include in the main alliance. This did not preclude the project team from dealing with non-alliance companies along the same principles as with the main alliance partners.

Example 2. An offshore gas compression platform included the compressor manufacturer, design contractor and offshore installation contractor as its alliance members. In this case, inclusion of the compressor manufacturer was essential as this single item had the largest impact on the functionality of the project. Equally importantly, both the designer and the installer depended greatly on the manufacturer to be able to deliver their accountabilities.

Owners may also be accustomed to utilising large contractors who offer skills and services and expertise over a wide, if not a full, range of activities in the realisation of a project. In many cases this is achieved through subcontracting major portions of the work. Frequently, these subcontractors themselves have valid and valuable expertise in managing and interfacing with other companies. The owner should therefore give careful consideration to the potential benefits that could be gained by contracting with these companies directly and including them in the alliance in their own right.

The issue of managing complexity and interfaces is an important one. Parties that are highly dependent on each other for their work should be prime candidates for inclusion, as effective management of complex interfaces is an important means of improving efficiency. This is especially relevant where there is a large labour element in their scopes. It is also consistent with the assertion that the alliance financial incentive scheme overcomes the limitations of traditional contracting described in Part 1 with respect to misalignment between different parties, and gives the participants a direct stake in managing interfaces efficiently.

Membership of the alliance will be determined at an early stage. Nevertheless, the possibility of adding new members at a later stage should be retained. The potential advantages and disadvantages of doing so should be kept under review, this being done jointly by all the original alliance members, as they will all have to give approval of the inclusion of new members.

4.3 Timing of selection

As has been repeated throughout this book, the selection of the alliance partners should take place as early as possible in the project time-frame in order to maximise the benefits of contractor expertise and to give parties sufficient time to become fully familiar with the project and thoroughly understand the risks that they are sharing with the other members. However, successful alliancing is just as dependent on the building of relationships. This takes time, and the early selection of contractors allows time for this to be done in parallel with the technical and other aspects of the work, and before the formal alliance is put in place and the project is faced with the heavy demands of the execution stage. Early selection also means that sufficient time is available to develop a solid commercial basis and to complete the various contracts, including the alliance agreement, thus providing a firm foundation for the project execution stage.

Figure 10 shows one approach to the timing of selection. In this example the selection of the alliance partners is spread over a period of time, with the engineering (design) contractor being the first to be selected. However, there have been cases where the owner has completed the selection and appointment of all the alliance partners at the start of the project definition phase. Figure 11 shows the sequence of activities required to finalise the commercial arrangements and contracts and should be read in conjunction with Figure 10.

It is acknowledged that there have been successful alliances set up both earlier and later than this timing. Later selection, however, is more likely to result in either the potential benefits not being fully realised or, as has been the case in some instances, a failure to meet expectations.

Example. An engineering contractor gave the example of one alliance that was not successful in meeting the agreed project goals. The fact that alliance partners were

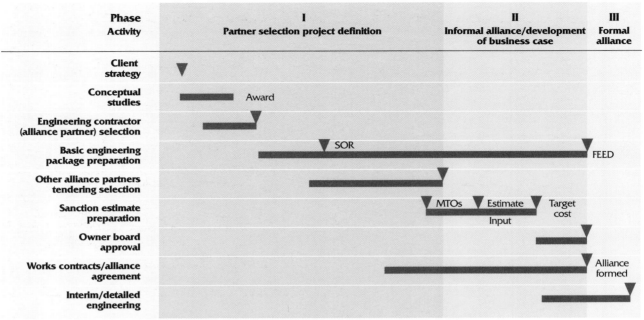

SOR, statement of requirements; FEED, front-end engineering and design package; MTO, material take-off.

Figure 10

The alliance partner
selection schedule

engaged after sanction and effectively had the cost estimate imposed on them was considered a major factor in the failure of the alliance. The ownership that is taken on during the preparation of the cost estimate and execution plan, before the owner has given final approval to proceed, generates significant commitment on the part of the corporate management of participating companies and project team to achieve or improve on the targets set.

4.4 Alliance partner selection process

As noted in Part 1, there are essentially three principal routes to selecting alliance partners:

■ open
■ restricted
■ negotiated.

All these routes are competitive or can be constructed to be so, and all could be used to select alliance partners.

However, the existence of specific circumstances such as:

■ a limited number of equivalent suppliers with long lead times and/or capacity constraints
■ highly specialised skills (including co-specialisation with the owner)
■ a previous successful relationship
■ a high level of interdependence with the owner or other parties that will participate

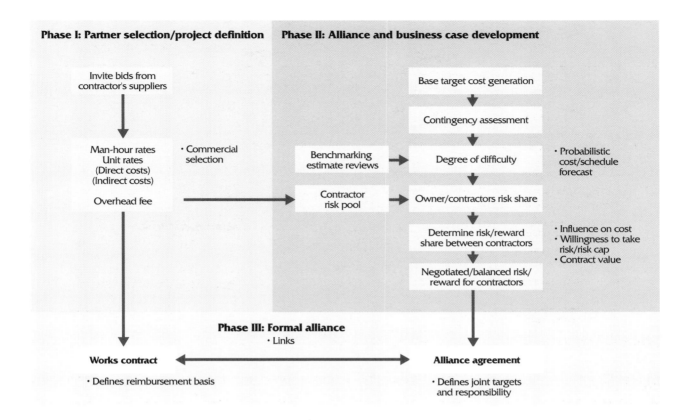

Phase I: Partner selection/project definition

Invite bids from contractor's suppliers

Man-hour rates
Unit rates
(Direct costs)
(Indirect costs)

Overhead fee

• Commercial selection

Phase II: Alliance and business case development

Base target cost generation

Contingency assessment

Benchmarking estimate reviews → Degree of difficulty

Contractor risk pool → Owner/contractors risk share

Determine risk/reward share between contractors

Negotiated/balanced risk/ reward for contractors

• Probabilistic cost/schedule forecast

• Influence on cost
• Willingness to take risk/risk cap
• Contract value

Phase III: Formal alliance
• Links

Works contract ⟷ **Alliance agreement**

• Defines reimbursement basis

• Defines joint targets and responsibility

Figure 11
The commercial
development model

indicate that a negotiated route is desirable, and it is recommended that the restricted route is chosen.

The reason for this recommendation is simply that requesting bids from a large number of contractors, many of whom may be either entirely unsuited to or unwilling to contemplate working in an alliance mode, would be counterproductive in terms of the effort required. In addition, many owners have found the restricted route to be particularly effective and appropriate for selecting alliance partners.

The restricted route is essentially a two-stage process.

Stage 1 is essentially a prequalification exercise, the results of which are used to establish a shortlist of contractors who will be invited to participate in a formal bid process. The number of companies to which the prequalification documents will be given depends on the specific alliance member being selected and the need to comply with any relevant legal or regulatory provisions.

The objectives of this prequalification stage should be two-fold:

■ to ensure that any contractor placed on the shortlist is fully competent to undertake the work involved

■ to establish that shortlisted contractors are willing, in principle, to enter into an alliancing arrangement.

It is recommended that the shortlist should comprise relatively few contractors, but that there be a sufficient number (say between three and six) to ensure that a competitive position is maintained.

Stage 2 is the bid process, which starts with the issue of the formal bid documents to the contractors shortlisted from Stage 1. As with traditional contractor selection processes, both technical and commercial criteria should be used and evaluated. However, Stage 2 is focused on identifying the contractor that will do the best job for the particular project, and in the context of alliancing this means that significant attention should to be given to assessing and evaluating the behavioural and cultural factors that are relevant to the alliancing approach.

Bids will usually request written responses, but it is recommended that the process includes provisions for these to be supplemented by some or all of the following:

■ formal dialogues
■ structured interviews with key corporate and project level personnel who will be involved in the project
■ interactive presentations.

These approaches should be specifically designed to gain information that supplements written responses, particularly in respect of corporate and cultural attitudes and individual behavioural aspects.

Figure 12

The 'coached' selection process

Some owners with experience in alliancing have also suggested that there is evidence that, as alliancing concepts have become more widely absorbed in the contracting culture, a tendency may have developed for so-called 'script writing' in written responses. The true content and intent of the contractor has to be verified, and the supplementary verbal procedures listed above offer a way to achieve this.

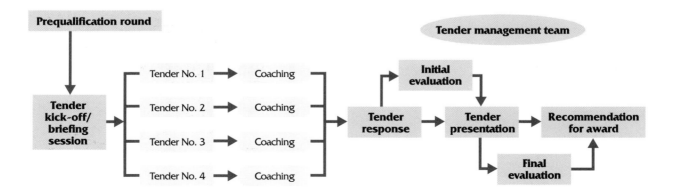

A concept termed 'coaching bids' has also been applied by some owners, and this should be given specific consideration when embarking on a selection process, especially when selecting from potential alliance partners that have no experience with the approach. The purpose of 'coaching bids' is simply to afford each contractor in the bid the maximum possibility of submitting the best bid he possibly can. Essentially, each contractor is given the opportunity to meet individually with the owner during the bid process, with the principal aim of enabling them to understand better the owner's requirements. Some owners that have used this approach have stated that it has proved valuable in terms of the quality of responses received.

There must be cognisance that this type of process does raise the issues of integrity, ethics and fair and equitable treatment. All these issues need to be addressed fully and taken into account in designing the details of the coaching process. Figure 12 shows the timing for the use of coaching in the tendering process.

4.5 Selection criteria

As noted in Part 1, owner organisations are entitled to select contractors competitively on the principle of best economic value. This is entirely complementary to the philosophy of alliancing in that it permits the owner to utilise non-price selection criteria if it considers these to be relevant in achieving the best economic value.

Clearly, the detailed selection criteria will depend on individual owner and project-specific circumstances, but in every case significant thought should be given to ensure that the chosen criteria are fully appropriate. Equally important is that all prequalification questionnaires and tender documents are structured in such a way that they will elicit information that is both relevant and pertinent to the chosen criteria.

Figure 13

An example of selection criteria weightings

As a rule, and to comply with relevant legislation, the owner should ensure that all criteria:

- are determined and fixed in advance of any part of the selection process
- are made known to those being invited to participate
- can be assessed objectively.

In broad terms the selection criteria will usually fall under one of the following headings:

- technical
- commercial
- alliancing related
- project specific.

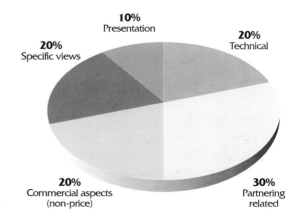

Technical
- Track record
- Technical competence
- Resource availability
- Nominated key personnel
- Local knowledge

Commercial – price
- Costs and rates
  - Reimbursable man-hour rates
  - Unit prices (material and labour)
  - Lump sums
- Overhead percentage required
- Profit level required

Specific views on project
- Organisation and methods
- Cost and schedule improvements
- Innovations

Alliancing related
- Alliancing philosophy and experience
- Company cultural aspects
- Corporate commitment and understanding
- Behavioural aspects
- Demonstrated commitment to project
- Views on improvement and innovation
- Flexibility

Commercial – non-price
- Contractual issues
- Appetite for risk share

Presentation
- Team dynamics
- Project manager, leadership skills
- Consistency with written proposal

Box 1

Criteria for alliance partner selection

Box 1 gives further details of some of the more specific aspects that would come under these broad headings. The relative importance of the different categories should be reflected by allocating them different weightings. Figure 13 shows an example of how weightings might be allocated to the various criteria listed in Box 1.

Table 2 illustrates the criteria and weightings actually used by an owner in a two-stage selection process, as described above. Of specific note in this example is the very low weighting attached to the commercial criterion in Stage 2. The owner reported that this was driven by specific market circumstances. The same owner and others have indicated that it is more common for commercial (price) considerations to comprise no more that 40–60% of the total score.

4.6 Evaluation plan and process

The owner should prepare a detailed evaluation plan in advance of starting any stage of a selection process. A properly constructed plan that is adhered to will ensure that all assessments and evaluations are objective and the risks of individual personal bias are removed.

As a minimum, the evaluation plan should incorporate:

Table 2

Example of criteria and weightings used

Criterion	Weighting (%)
Stage 1: Prequalification	
Track record	27.5
Competence to provide service required	10.0
Workload capacity	5.0
Facilities and resources	4.5
Quality management	9.0
HSE policy	9.0
Continuous performance improvement	6.0
Ability to meet owner's 'conditions of satisfaction'	5.5
Commitment to work in an alliance	13.5
Total	**100**
Stage 2: Bid	
Behaviours and attitudes	25
Team members	21
Competence and innovation	18
Systems	14
Track record	11
Organisation	7
Commercial	4
Total	**100**
HSE, Health and Safety Executive.	

- details of the evaluation process
  - schedules for evaluation execution
  - evaluation team, including individual accountabilities
  - procedures to ensure confidentiality
  - internal (owner) review and approval processes
- selection criteria
- details of the scoring system, including the weighting attached to each criterion
- detailed guidelines on how those doing the evaluation are to evaluate the responses.

Where appropriate, the evaluation plan and scoring system should include the written proposals and the subsequent post-tender interviews and presentations.

In all cases specific checks should be made to ensure that all selection processes comply with applicable legislation, directives and other regulatory requirements, and the final version of the evaluation plan should be agreed with all interested parties of the owner, such as its tender boards or committee, legal department and internal audit functions.

It is recommended that, wherever possible, evaluation and scoring should initially be carried out independently by more than one member of the evaluation team. Any marked differences between individual assessments should be thoroughly investigated before final scores are allocated. This will help ensure the objectivity of the process. It is particularly important that the way in which apparently subjective factors are to be evaluated is carefully thought through, so that they can in fact be evaluated objectively.

Example. A criterion may be senior management commitment to and understanding of alliancing. This criterion could be evaluated using a list of issues and a set of scores related to predetermined model responses. Actual responses would be compared to models and a score allocated accordingly. In general terms a score of zero would equate to 'Contractor offered no evidence that he indicated commitment to the concept or to demonstrate understanding of it'. The maximum score would equate to 'Contractor offers solid evidence to show that he is committed to the concept and to demonstrate a good understanding of alliance principles through statements within the written proposal and discussion of the issues during interviews'.

Another aspect of the valuation system that needs to be carefully thought through is how commercial aspects will be combined with all the other criteria. One possible approach to this is first to evaluate all the criteria, with the exception of specific price data. The specific price data are taken as an absolute, but are modified by the score allocated to all the other criteria, and this modified score is used to finalise the rankings of the competing contractor.

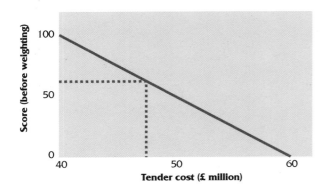

Another approach is to have a predetermined system for converting prices or costs into scores – a cost conversion graph. Such graphs are usually constructed to take on the basis of what would be expected to be reasonable costs, taking into account current market conditions and recent costs for similar services and the range of prices or budget costs that it is anticipated the contractors might submit. Scores allocated to each contractor using this graph are then aggregated with the scores against all other criteria and using the agreed weightings allocated to each. Figure 14 shows an example of a cost conversion graph.

Figure 14

An example of a cost conversion graph

One final point worth noting is that, whichever approach is adopted, it should not be assumed that contractors are giving an irrevocable commitment to entering a formal alliance agreement for the execution phase. That can only come when full contractual and commercial details for the alliance have been determined.

5. Contracts for alliancing

Summary

This section provides discussion and guidance on key issues relating to contracts for an alliance.

Alternative contract structures are outlined. One of these – a combination of individual works contracts between the owner and each of the other members of the alliance, and a single alliance agreement covering all the members including the owner – is used as a framework for identifying and discussing the key issues related to each.

The purpose and contents of each of the two contacts are outlined, and key points relating to the relationship they have to each other are highlighted.

Appropriate advice and input should always be sought from legally qualified personnel when constructing contracts for an alliance.

Contents

- **Contractual structures for alliances**
- **Relationship of works contracts and alliance agreement**
- **Tax and corporate implications of alliancing**
- **Works contracts**
  Compensation and reimbursement terms
  Supervening insolvency
  Information management, intellectual property and confidentiality
  Audit and inspection
  Early warning and joint problem-solving
  Snagging and rework
  Choice of law
- **Alliance agreement**
  Objectives of the alliance
  Relationships and organisational structure
  – Principles governing working relationships
  – Alliance board
  – Disputes resolution
  – Integrated project management team
  Incentive scheme
  – Purpose
  – Performance measurement criteria
  – Shares in gainshare
  – Changes to targets for performance measurement criteria
  – Procedure for agreeing changes to targets
  – Definition of project completion
  – Calculation of final cost
  – Calculation of gainshare
  Other important contractual issues
  – Circumstances for excluding an alliance member
  – Overriding works contracts provisions
  – Integrated teams – secondment of personnel
  – Indemnities
  – No partnership
  – Release
  – Confidentiality
  Other clauses

5.1 Contractual structures for alliances

As for any project, the contractual arrangements between the parties in an alliance must first recognise that there is a need to make provision to ensure the physical delivery of the project in accordance with the requirements of the owner. In addition, there needs to be expression of the specific aspects of the alliancing arrangement.

Figure 15

An example of a partnering charter

In partnering the specific aspects of the partnering arrangement are usually given expression in a partnering charter, which is not legally binding. An example of a partnering charter is shown in Figure 15.

XYZ Project

Partnering Charter

This Charter sets out the understandings reached by the participants at the XYZ Partnering Workshop held on 22 September 2000. Although this Charter is not intended to have formal legal standing, by their signature the parties are committed to the spirit and intent of its provisions in the interests of the successful completion of the XYZ Project.

MISSION STATEMENT

Our Mission is to complete the project with a satisfactory outcome for all parties client, contractors, subcontractors and suppliers alike.

OBJECTIVES

The satisfaction of our Mission will require that:

- The project is completed within its budget and that each participant achieve this financial goal
- That the project is completed within its original schedule
- That the project fully meets its operational requirements
- That the project is completed with zero accidents
- That the participants are able to reflect on the project experience as rewarding and satisfying
- That should appropriate circumstances arise the parties would wish to work with each other again

BEHAVIOURAL REQUIREMENTS

To achieve these objectives we commit to:

- Recognise, respect and promote each others' aims and interests
- Align these aims and interests with the project objectives
- Conduct our relationship in a spirit of specific cooperation and mutual respect
- Respond to difficulties from whatever source in a positive, understanding and constructive manner without the attachment of blame
- Strive to avoid disputes by resolving issues openly and early
- Encourage flexibility and innovation in all matters

Signed

_____ Ivor Winter NMOP Company

_____ Val Barns PRM Contractors

_____ Bob Jones Piping Incorporated

_____ John Smith XYZ Steel Workers

_____ Steven Dawes MWPL Contractors

_____ Alan Downs BRLT Company

Signed at XYZ Project Partnering Meeting on 22nd day of September 2000

In an alliance, the specific aspects are invariably incorporated in a legally binding contract, and various options are available in respect of the overall contractual structure which may be used. The most common options are:

(a) Standard contracts (referred to in this book as 'works contracts') between the owner and each of the contractors in the alliance are used to cover the physical delivery of the project, and an alliance agreement is used to cover the alliance arrangements. All the parties in the alliance are signatories to the alliance agreement.

(b) A single legally binding contract or agreement which covers both the physical delivery of the project and all aspects of the alliance arrangement between the parties.

Option (a) above is the one most commonly adopted, as it offers a pragmatic approach that can simplify the process of negotiating and finalising the contractual arrangements. However, the legal acceptability of such an arrangement may be open to question in some countries, and the parties may themselves have a preference for a single contract. In both these cases option (b) can be used.

Option (a), which is illustrated diagrammatically in Figure 16, is used to highlight and discuss they key issues relating to the contracts, which are covered in more detail in the rest of this section. Nevertheless, the majority of the issues raised and discussed will still be relevant to option (b).

Figure 16

The contractual framework for an alliance

Whichever option is chosen, legal advice and input should always be sought.

5.2 Relationship of works contracts and alliance agreement

It is important to recognise from the outset that the works contracts and the alliance agreement effectively deal with entirely separate matters. Consequently, they are most appropriately viewed as 'stand-alone' agreements. From this perspective, there should be no conflict or inconsistency between them and questions of 'precedence' should not arise. Nevertheless, it may be prudent to include wording in the alliance agreement which makes it clear that the existence of the alliance agreement does not impinge on any of the rights and obligations of the parties in respect of the works contracts.

In summary, the works contracts:

- define the services to be provided by the contractor
- establish the rights and obligations of the owner and the contractor
- define functionality, quality and other appropriate requirements
- provide for payments to the contractor for goods and/or services provided
- incorporate specific and general terms and conditions.

The alliance agreement:

- defines the details of the incentive scheme which links the parties' rewards to the total project outcome

and in most cases it also:

- expresses the 'objective' of the alliance
- details the 'principles' which will govern the working relationship of the parties

■ establishes any organisational structures specifically related to the alliancing arrangement (e.g. many alliance agreements make provision for the establishment of a so-called alliance board which is composed of senior executives of the parties).

Where the parties have so agreed, the alliance agreement may also contain provisions that override some of the specific terms and conditions of the works contracts, for as long as the alliance agreement continues to be in force.

Despite the different nature of the two agreements, there are inevitably some links between them which need to be considered and, where appropriate, catered for in one or other or both of the agreements. Some of these potential links are discussed below.

5.3 Tax and corporate implications of alliancing

Although alliances are usually intended to be purely contractual and behavioural in nature, there may be a risk that the relationship is interpreted as creating a new legal entity such as a partnership or joint venture. This could give rise to issues relating to compliance with laws regulating the formation of such entities. The alliance agreement in particular often includes a clause or clauses clarifying that the alliance is not a legal entity. Tax issues may also arise, and advice should be taken on a case-by-case basis.

5.4 Works contracts for partnering and alliancing

5.4.1 General

Works contracts may be based on either standard or bespoke forms of contract. The use of standard forms of contract can help to reduce tendering and contract administration costs. Whichever form is used, it should be thoroughly reviewed to ensure that any clause that would or could conflict or interfere with the alliancing process is suitably modified.

In amending standard forms of contract or preparing bespoke forms, particular attention should be given to clauses relating to:

■ giving notices
■ resolving disputes
■ controlling information and communication.

Other issues that frequently lead to initial differences of view among the parties include provisions dealing with:

■ liquidated damages
■ warranties and defects liability

- rework
- retentions.

Potential participants in an alliance may take the view that alliancing means that many of these provisions should either be deleted or substantially modified from what would normally be incorporated. However, this is highly dependent on the view taken of how risks are to be managed and shared.

In principle, there is no reason why the underlying work(s) contracts terms should differ substantially from contracts used hitherto. From a pragmatic point of view, there is merit in agreeing terms and conditions that would be considered appropriate if there were no alliance agreement in place and then to deal specifically with any agreed modifications in the alliance agreement (see Part 2, Section 5.5.4).

5.4.2 Compensation or reimbursement terms

In alliancing, there are three main factors to consider in relation to works contract remuneration terms and these are all related to there being an incentive scheme through which the parties will share the benefits of any cost savings and the risks of costs being exceeded.

- *Maximising the opportunities for cost savings.* It is recognised that, in most cases, a substantial proportion of the total project spend will be with contractors and suppliers who are not included in the alliance and hence the incentive scheme. However, the direct spend with the parties to the alliance will itself be a significant proportion of the total, and so it is important that the possibility of achieving cost savings in this area is not precluded.
- *Focusing each of the alliance members on their own performance as well as that of others.* The initial, and perhaps understandable, attitude of those invited to participate in an alliance incentive scheme is that any savings will come, not from their own performance improvements, but from other sources. The evidence from successful alliances quite clearly demonstrates that this is not so, and that significant gains can be achieved by the members themselves, including the owner.
- *Giving practical effect to the incentive scheme.* The notional basis of the incentive scheme is that each of the members will put a specified sum of money at stake. It is therefore important to ensure that, in the event that the agreed target cost is exceeded, each of the members does not continue to generate profit that will be offsetting their share of any overrun.

The simplest and most effective way of achieving all three objectives is to adopt what is frequently referred to an 'open-book' approach to remuneration within the works contracts, which take the following (ideal) shape:

■ The costs of all goods and services provided are reimbursed at direct cost, excluding all overhead and profit elements.

■ Direct project overheads are overhead costs and other costs (e.g. computers, office accommodation, telephones) that can be attributed directly to the project.

■ Corporate overheads.

■ Profit.

The profit element should be set at a fixed sum based on the individual contractor's profit expectations and estimated (predicted) direct costs for his scope, as included in the incentive scheme target cost. Fixing profit in this way ensures that the individual contractor does not continue to generate profit via the works contract to offset risk payments if the target cost is exceeded.

Ideally, the corporate overhead element should also be set at a fixed sum in a similar manner. The argument for this is simply that the corporate overhead element is usually based on a business plan which envisages that the company's total corporate overheads will be covered from a certain level of activity spread over a number of different contracts. Consequently, it seems unreasonable that alliance partners should benefit through an increased corporate overhead recovery resulting from performance poorer than that implied in their estimate for their scope.

The argument for fixing the direct project overhead is weaker in that it is a direct consequence of undertaking the project. Nevertheless, it is worth considering, and some alliances have chosen to do so.

While it is recognised that contractors will, inevitably, see a risk in this approach, there is a potential upside in it for them in that if they complete their scope at lower direct cost then the profit and overhead recovery is effectively higher in terms of resources employed.

5.4.3 Supervening insolvency

Insolvency of one of the parties continues to be a risk in alliancing, just as it is under other forms of construction contract. It must be considered when taking a decision whether to dispense with bonding or performance guarantees in the works contracts. This is particularly so where, as is sometimes the case in such relationships, the owner funds the contractor on an immediate basis, in order to reduce the project costs overall.

5.4.4 Information management, intellectual property and confidentiality

The aims of partnering and alliancing in relation to information exchange generally require that all parties should have timely and open information that is relevant for them. In some cases integrated document-handling systems are used.

In the public sector, this may raise issues of audit acceptability or even state security, and in certain sectors (such as transport or power) it is likely to attract attention from safety regulators. In all cases it raises certain contractual issues:

- confidentiality and intellectual property (discussed further below)
- compatibility of actual information flows with contract requirements and dispute resolution arrangements
- respect for legal requirements (e.g. UK data protection legislation).

Openness does not mean ignoring the requirements of confidentiality and security or concerns regarding management of publicity. The parties should have a clear understanding of what information will be shared and what it can legitimately be used for. This should be supported by:

- enforceable contractual arrangements
- procedures within each organisation to ensure that employees understand and respect limitations on the sharing and use of information.

In some cases, because of the scope and nature of the information that is shared, contract terms concerning confidentiality may need to be more rigorous in partnering and alliancing than in conventional contracts.

Intellectual property is relevant for partnering and alliancing in a number of ways:

- it may be created where the relationship promotes innovation
- parties may bring their own intellectual property to the relationship
- the project may make use of the intellectual property of third parties.

Where new intellectual property is or may be created, the parties should clearly understand who will own what rights to the intellectual property. (For example, it may be owned by the contractor, with a view to exploitation in the market and with the owner having all the intellectual property licences necessary for ongoing operation of the project. Alternatively, it may be owned by the owner, who will use it to operate the project, but with the contractor having a licence which permits its application in defined circumstances elsewhere.)

Where parties bring their own intellectual property to the relationship, it should be clearly understood how the intellectual property can be applied by others in relation to the project, and any restrictions on its use should be protected (as with confidentiality) by:

- enforceable contractual arrangements which reflect the agreed understanding
- procedures within each organisation to ensure that employees understand and respect limitations on the sharing and use of the intellectual property concerned.

Where third party intellectual property is used, it should be clearly understood who takes responsibility for the terms on which the intellectual property is made available (i.e. for the existence of and any limitations on rights to use it). Contractually, the parties may wish to protect their individual positions by indemnities as they would on a conventional project.

5.4.5 Audit and inspection

In some alliances audit and inspection by the owner is reduced to a minimum, and in some instances even eliminated, partly as means of reducing costs. Such arrangements are unlikely to be acceptable in the public sector and the majority of owners are unlikely to accept complete elimination of such audits. As an alternative, audit and inspection may be carried out jointly or by independent consultants, whose costs are shared. Subcontractors and suppliers may also be parties to such arrangements.

The works contracts should be the primary vehicle for covering this issue. If considered appropriate, any modifications to these arising from the decision to form an alliance can be covered in the alliance agreement.

5.4.6 Early warning and joint problem-solving

Addressing and seeking joint solutions to problems is an important aspect of successful alliances. This will often be covered in the 'principles' embodied in the alliance agreement. However, it could be helpful to insert appropriate provisions in the works contracts as well which oblige the parties to give each other early warning of problems with time, cost, quality or safety consequences and an obligation to address them jointly.

5.4.7 Snagging and rework

The usual practice is to incorporate standard provisions in the works contract(s) covering rework that is found to be necessary. Provisions obliging the parties to cooperate to identify defects, to programme remedial works and to agree work methods, including acceptable alternatives, should be included.

The question of how rework will be paid for also needs to be addressed. In some alliances, the cost of rework has been carried out on a cost-reimbursable basis, either with or without profit, while in others it has been to the sole cost of the particular alliance participant. Where the cost of rework is reimbursed the costs so incurred are normally taken into account in calculating the final cost for the purposes of the incentive scheme.

5.4.8 Choice of law

The choice of law should be consistent with any dispute-resolution arrangements. Where the law chosen is not the law of the country in which the project will be implemented, care needs to be taken to ensure that:

- the project will be implemented in conformity with the applicable law of the country of implementation (e.g. it will conform to applicable planning, zoning and environmental laws)
- ancillary obligations (e.g. in relation to working hours or use of labour) are consistent with the applicable law in the country of implementation
- where relevant, the terms of the contract would not offend against applicable law or public policy in the country of implementation or in any country where dispute resolution is likely to take place.

5.5 Alliance agreement

The purpose of this section is to highlight the key issues that it is suggested should be covered by the alliance agreement. These issues are largely discussed in terms of general principles. Some issues relating to the alliance agreement incentive scheme are discussed in more detailed and practical terms in Part 2, Section 6.

5.5.1 Objective(s) of the alliance

Experience suggests that it is always worth incorporating a simple statement of the objective(s) of the alliance as this can be used to help focus the parties on the fact that the main driver for setting up an alliance is to deliver improved performance.

In most instances this will be a simple statement that the objective is to improve on the agreed performance criteria targets embodied in the incentive scheme. If some important issues (e.g. quality, safety) are not a direct part of the incentive scheme the objective(s) will often be written to make it clear that these are not to be sacrificed in the pursuit of rewards.

5.5.2 Relationships and organisational structures

Principles governing working relationships

It is extremely important that the principles that will govern and guide the way in which the parties will work together and behave so as to achieve the objective(s) are clearly set out in the alliance agreement. It is equally important that these principles are not simply imposed by the owner, but are jointly developed and agreed by and between the parties. Experience has indicated that this is an important facet of building and establishing the relationship between them and the commitment of all the parties. Put another way, *the process and the product are equally important.*

Alliance board

Purpose and role

The majority of alliances choose to establish a so-called alliance board. Where this is the case a key issue to be addressed is whether or not the board has executive powers in respect of implementing the project. The principal arguments in favour of the alliance board having executive powers are:

- ■ that this is totally in line with the notion of working together to achieve common objectives
- ■ if contractors have a financial stake (via the risk/reward scheme) then they need to have the right to take part in the decision-making process.

A number of alliance agreements have included provisions for the alliance board to make executive decisions in a relatively wide range of topics. Several have also included detailed provisions as to how such decisions will be reached, including voting procedures in the event of lack of unanimity. In most instances, however, there has usually been a provision giving the owner the ultimate right to make a decision unilaterally (a veto right).

This latter provision was essentially a recognition of the rights conferred on the owner in the works contracts. However, the inclusion of such provisions can, or could, create an expectation that the alliance board, rather than the owner, will control the project and approve variation orders, etc. Such provisions could also lead to confusion in respect of liabilities and other matters in the event of a dispute arising under the works contracts.

To avoid these potential problems, full recognition should be given to the 'separateness' of the works contracts. In order to maintain the concept of individual corporate accountability, it is now a more usual practice to make it clear that the purpose and role of the board is 'to provide advice, guidance and support to the owner in connection with achieving the objective(s)'.

It is recognised that some potential alliance members may have difficulty in accepting this concept. However, experience shows that the vast majority ultimately recognise that 'He who pays the piper calls the tine' and will be willing to accept this approach, provided that the owner gives them confidence that their skills expertise and knowledge are valued, that they will be able to contribute these via the alliance board and that the owner will take account of their views. Such confidence may be given by incorporating appropriate items in the 'principles'.

It is also worth noting that, in practice, the alliance board meetings often provide a convenient opportunity for the parties to agree various matters. However, in contractual terms, it will be the owner who takes the action necessary to give effect to such decisions, and it is important to maintain the distinction between the parties deciding matters and the advice and support given by the alliance board.

Composition

The usual and recommended practice is that all alliance board members (including the owner's) are senior executives or managers of the parties who are not directly involved in managing the execution of the project on a day-to-day basis. Insofar as the owner is concerned, there can be significant merit in his alliance board representative being a senior business manager holding accountability for the business outcome of the project, rather than a project professional such as the project manager. In practice it is likely that key project personnel will attend alliance board meetings on an invitational basis.

Payments for board members

To avoid any confusion, the agreement should include explicit provision as to whether or not board members are to be reimbursed for their participation in board meetings and activities associated with the board. There are no strong arguments as to whether or not alliance board members should be reimbursed, but if payments are to be made it is recommended that these are covered in the works contracts.

Disputes resolution

The avoidance or early resolution of disputes is one of the intended outcomes of alliancing. The extent to which this is achieved will be a measure of the success or otherwise of the arrangement. The ethos of alliancing, the emphasis on openness and trust, the alignment of objectives and the 'no blame' culture all combine to make it less likely that alliance projects will be disputatious. For these reasons many alliances (particularly where the participants are experienced in the technique) have not included detailed formal provision for the resolution of disputes. Many, however, have included a general obligation within the 'principles' for the parties to work together to resolve any issues or problems that do arise. The alliance board can play an important role in this regard.

There is merit in promoting the resolution of issues and problems at the lowest level possible within the project team itself. Where this has been the case, the experience has been that there have been very few cases where resolution within the project has not been possible. For those issues that have not been resolved in the project the alliance board has been able to resolve the matters, thus avoiding further escalation of the issue or problem.

However, disputes can always arise and there may be those who wish to incorporate a more formal and structured approach to dispute avoidance and resolution. Numerous techniques are available for avoidance and resolution, which should make resort to litigation a rarity. These techniques are described in more detail in Appendix 1.

Integrated project management team and project alliance leadership team

A number of alliance agreements have contained detailed provisions related to the establishment of an integrated project management team. Concerns have been raised that the wording of these provisions may create the erroneous expectation that the company was limiting its discretion under the works contracts by delegating and/or sharing authority.

To avoid this, some recent alliance agreements have embodied the concept of a project alliance leadership team. Like the alliance board, the project alliance leadership team has no executive authority in respect of the overall management of the project. The idea is that the project alliance leadership team will be a forum within the project in which all the parties have the right, and indeed duty, to express their views and ideas on how the project can deliver the best results for all the parties. The project alliance leadership team will also be charged with reviewing and monitoring on a regular ongoing basis whether or not the 'principles' are actually being applied at the working level.

If a project alliance leadership team is established it usually comprises the senior representatives from each of the parties who are working on the project on a day-to-day basis. It should be noted that the project alliance leadership team is not intended to cut across the notion of creating an integrated project management team along the models which have been a powerful force in successful alliances. That approach is still considered to be valid and valuable, and indeed a key feature of successful alliances. If thought desirable and agreed by the parties, the intent behind forming an integrated project team approach could be incorporated in the 'principles'.

5.5.3 Incentive scheme

The incentive scheme is at the heart of the alliance agreement. It is vitally important that the details of the incentive scheme are thoroughly thought through and that the end result as expressed in the alliance agreement is clear and unambiguous.

There are a number of specific issues that need to be covered, and these are described below. However, it also important that the fundamental purpose of the incentive scheme is appreciated.

Purpose of incentive scheme

The fundamental purpose of the incentive scheme is to achieve alignment between the interests of the company and those of the alliance members, as opposed to the misalignment which usually occurred in traditional contracting approaches. Alignment of interests is primarily achieved by constructing the incentive scheme such that:

- there is a direct link between reward and the total outcome of the project, rather than to an individual contractor's performance
- the alliance members have more to gain through the scheme by efficient joint (with the owner) execution of the project than through leveraging their own position via their individual works contract.

This is designed to encourage cooperation and collaboration to devise and implement more efficient ways to execute the project.

Performance measurement criteria

Note: The word 'gainshare' is used in this section to denote the amount of money that will be payable as a result of the operation of the incentive scheme.

General

Each individual project has to determine appropriate criteria against which performance will be measured and the gainshare calculated and paid. Performance criteria should be:

- directly linked to what would make that project a 'success' for the owner
- be 'final outcome' measures
- criteria which either directly generate added value or detract from value
- simple (complicated criteria should be avoided)
- unambiguous
- easily measurable
- incapable of being manipulated by any party, including the owner.

Possible criteria

Capital cost

Capital cost will invariably be one of the performance criteria. The simple principle that is applied is that the owner and the other participants will share the results of any underrun or overrun against a pre-agreed target cost.

The main issue around capital cost is related to what the target cost should be and how any overruns against this target will be shared. The most usual approach is that owner and contractor(s) will share any overrun to a pre-agreed formula up to an agreed level of overrun, after which the owner takes all the risk. Essentially this provides a cap on the contractor's risk. On the other hand, there is usually no limit on how much the contractors can benefit from savings.

Project schedule

Schedules should only be used as criteria if early or late completion adds or destroys value for the owner (e.g. early completion allows the owner to generate value from the use of the facility or even from another source). In most instances, the owner will be unwilling to have schedule gainshare linked directly to the additional value creation (e.g. the profit generated by sales of a product). Clearly, what the owner is willing to offer by way of incentive payments should still be related to the additional value created. Risk payments in the event of late delivery should similarly be related to the value destroyed.

It should be noted that there are projects where early delivery does not offer the possibility of generating additional value, but at the same time value can be destroyed if the project is late. In such cases it would be entirely appropriate for the owner to propose a risk-only formula. Contractors may be reluctant to accept such a proposal, but if it is linked to waiving 'liquidated damages' provisions in the works contracts, they may then essentially regard this as a reclassification of risk.

Quality and reliability

Quality and reliability are always important issues for an owner. However, whether or not they should be used as specific criteria for measuring performance and determining gainshare should be carefully examined.

Quality and reliability will usually be addressed and prescribed both in the works contracts and in contracts with other third parties for the supply of goods and services in connection with the project. These contracts will usually contain remedies for failure to meet quality and/or reliability requirements. These provisions, together with the proper (and owner audited) application of quality assurance and quality control procedures, should probably be viewed as the prime route to achieving the owner's requirement in respect of quality and reliability.

Nevertheless, there is a case for linking the payment of gainshare to demonstrating that the project as delivered is actually capable of doing what it was designed to do. This can be achieved via the definition of 'project completion' for the purposes of the alliance agreement, which can incorporate the achievement of satisfactory test runs to prove design capacities and other critical design criteria over a limited time period (see Part 2, Section 6).

It is recognised that this approach can only give an indication of quality and reliability, but nevertheless it goes some way to limiting the risk to the company of paying gainshare for a plant that does not meet quality and reliability requirements.

Safety and environmental performance

Safety and environmental performance are also extremely important issues for the owner, and there is unlikely to be any argument that excellent performance in these areas is an objective for all the participants in a project. However, it is questionable whether safety and environmental performance should be used as specific and direct gainshare criteria, although it is recognised that there are divergent views on this both within owner and contractor organisations.

Although it is clear that failure to deliver acceptable performance in these areas can destroy value, this is unlikely to be directly measurable. On the other hand, putting a gainshare mechanism in place would effectively ascribe a value to them. While this may appear reasonable, it could lead to political and/or public relations problems (e.g. an outsider could argue that the gainshare mechanism means that the owner, and indeed the contractors, value a life at a certain monetary value).

There is also the problem of constructing mechanisms that are win–win for the owner and contractors. Most mechanisms proposed penalise the contractors by reducing or eliminating gainshare. It can be argued that this effectively means that the owner gains because he does not have to pay out gainshare.

Essentially the debate centres around whether or not offering incentives to companies at the corporate level is the most appropriate approach to achieving the desired ends. Some projects have taken the view that it is, while others have chosen to address these issues outside the incentive scheme (e.g. some projects have set up separately funded incentive schemes that are aimed at the personnel (at all levels) involved in the project) and some have taken the view that neither is appropriate.

Life-cycle and operating costs

Life-cycle costs are of increasing concern to businesses since the capital cost can represent a relatively small percentage of the total cost of ownership of a facility over its lifetime. Many alliances have chosen not to incentivise life-cycle costs because of the difficulties of measuring them and the perception that some alliance members have little or no influence over them. However, there are examples where there has been an element of gainshare related to life-cycle and operating costs.

Intermediate milestones

Some owners have chosen to link gainshare to performance measured against pre-agreed intermediate milestones. While it is appreciated that managing against such intermediate milestones can be a valuable project management tool, this approach is not recommended unless the achievement or non-achievement gives an inherent and directly measurable benefit or loss to the owner. This is because linking gainshare to intermediate milestones:

■ potentially restricts the freedom of the parties to do what is best in terms of achieving the best overall results
■ conflicts with the principle that gainshare payments are primarily about directly linking rewards to overall project incomes.

For example, it is not inconceivable that there could be a failure to meet intermediate milestones yet still bring the project in at lower than the target cost and ahead of the target completion date. So, although the owner would have gained from this position, the contractors' share would be reduced simply because of not meeting some intermediate milestone.

An example of when the use of an intermediate milestone might be appropriate would be where bringing part of a facility into production earlier than the overall facility has the capability of allowing the owner to generate value. Even here, however, the way in which the gainshare mechanism works as a whole has to be given careful consideration. For example, any gains from early completion of a part of the facility might be entirely wiped out by loses arising from cost and/or schedule overruns for the total facility.

Shares in gainshare

The alliance agreement should clearly document the shares or interest that each of the parties has in the incentive scheme.

Circumstances in which targets for performance criteria can be changed

It is an absolute imperative that the circumstances in which changes to target performance criteria can be made are clearly and unambiguously described in the alliance agreement.

Procedure for agreeing changes to targets

A clear procedure for agreeing any changes to the target performance criteria should be set out in the alliance agreement. To avoid unnecessary and costly accounting processes, it is recommended that the procedure is worded to encourage the parties to agree the changes based on the estimated impact rather than on the actual impact.

Definition of project completion

A definition of project completion is required for the purposes of triggering the calculation and payment of gainshare. This definition is quite separate from, and usually different from, that contained in works contracts. There is considerable merit in defining project completion in a way that enables the owner to ascertain that a completed and 'working' project, which meets the defined functionality criteria, has been delivered.

The majority of recent alliances have adopted the concept of achievement of 'beneficial operation' or 'beneficial use' to define the completion, this being a point at which the facilities are producing revenue-generating products. This concept has the double advantage of:

- bringing focus to the real objective of the project
- encouraging the integration of operational input and involvement in the project, as it also embraces commissioning of the facilities.

Calculation of final cost

Definition of what is included in final cost

It is necessary to provide a clear definition of what is to be included in the final cost.

Usually this will be simply the sum of all costs invoiced and paid for under the works contracts and under all other contracts for the supply of goods and services for the project. It will also include the owner's costs if these have been included in the target cost, which is recommended.

It may be desirable to define final cost in such a way that it can be agreed, even though not all the final invoices are to hand. This has the advantage of allowing for the possibility of concluding the determination of gainshare at the earliest possible date. This would mean that part of the final cost would be an estimate of costs yet to be invoiced and paid.

There are also some technical issues relating to insurance that need to be addressed. For example, if a common construction all-risks policy is to be effected, then the implications of this in respect of defining and (calculating) the final cost need to be covered.

Procedure for calculating final cost

This is essentially a detailed timetable and procedure for the process of calculating and agreeing the final cost, and from that the gainshare.

Expert procedure

It is always possible that the parties will be unable to agree the final cost calculation, and to cover this eventuality it may be advisable to include an 'expert procedure' as a means of resolving such disagreements.

It should be noted, however, that the expert should not be given any remit in respect of resolving any matters that are governed by the works contracts (e.g. a dispute around a variation or change in an order) or on other matters relating to matters covered in the alliance agreement (e.g. determining whether or not performance criteria have been met). The expert's role should be simply that of ascertaining that the final cost has included all the costs that should properly be taken into account and that the calculation has been done accurately.

Calculation of gainshare

General

A clear and precise mechanism (formula) for how gainshare will be calculated against each of the performance criteria is required. As noted earlier (see Part 2, Section 5.2) it is recommended that a separate gainshare mechanism be constructed for each criterion and the results for each aggregated to determine the total gainshare.

In constructing the mechanisms a number of issues have (or may have) to be addressed, including.

- agreeing the target
- the shares (interests) of each party
- agreeing any limitations (caps)
- the level of overrun at which all of the contractor's risk money is 'recovered' by the owner (cost criteria)
- the relative values of gainshare for each criterion
- whether or not there should be a range of outcomes around the target at which no gainshare is payable either on the upside or the downside.

Limitations (caps)

The usual approach is that the risk to the contractors in respect of gainshare will be limited (capped) at some mutually agreed level. However, where there are several gainshare criteria, it may be appropriate to have an individual limitation on each or some of the criteria. This would be applied prior to aggregating gainshare against all the criteria and then applying the overall limitation.

A further issue is that, occasionally, the owner may seek to limit the amount the contractors can earn on the upside. This usually derives from a concern that the target cost may be 'too easy'. However, before pressing for such a limitation it is worth considering what impact this might have on the contractors' attitudes and whether this would really be in the owner's ultimate interest.

5.5.4 Other important contractual issues

Circumstances under which a party may be 'excluded' from the agreement

It is advisable to incorporate clear and express provisions in the agreement regarding the circumstances under which a contractor can be excluded ('excluded' in this sense means removed) from the alliance. There are a number of views on how this should be handled, and there are two principal issues involved:

- What are the circumstances under which exclusion should be possible?
- Who should have the right to exclude a party?

Circumstances

Essentially there are two points of view: one is that the circumstances should cover a breakdown in 'relationships' between two (or more) of the parties; and other is that exclusion should be linked directly to termination of a contracting party's works contract. The former view is based on the possibility that two parties could find themselves unable to work together in a meaningful way, but at the same time there is no wish or desire to terminate either of the parties' works contract. The latter is based on the view that, once committed to an alliance, none of the parties should be able to leave except under the most exceptional circumstances.

Right to exclude

The debate here centres around whether exclusion should be the sole right of the owner or whether such a decision should be dependent on the unanimous agreement of all the parties other than the one whose exclusion is being considered. The former could be construed as 'fettering' the rights of the owner, as discussed above, and pragmatically it would be extremely unlikely that an owner would go the lengths of excluding a contractor without consulting other parties to the agreement.

Overriding works contracts provisions

Contractors will frequently press for certain provisions of the works contracts to be overridden by the alliance agreement. These are usually risk- or liability-related provisions. Careful consideration needs to be given before acceding to such requests.

It is not possible to anticipate everything that may be raised, but two of the most common issues that arise in this context are:

■   liquidated damages (if these are included in the works contracts)
■   rework.

Including a clause that overrides any liquidated damages in the works contracts can be justified if one of the performance criteria in the alliance agreement is the schedule. The argument is that to do otherwise means that the contractors who are parties to the alliance agreement face a possibility of being penalised twice for the same thing.

The argument in favour of overriding the works contracts provisions on rework essentially turns on the notion that to do so:

■   promotes the concept of a 'no blame culture'
■   is consistent with the concept of sharing of risks.

While the former has some merit, the latter presupposes that it is the intent in an alliance to share all risks. A more logical approach is that the intent is to share risks that are not within the sole control of one of the individual parties. From this perspective, overriding the rework provisions becomes less tenable.

It can also be argued that overriding these provisions:

■   exposes all the other parties to a the risk that one party will consistently fail in terms of the quality of his own work without being exposed to the full consequences of doing so (i.e. the costs will be shared with all the other parties through the incentive scheme)
■   are a disincentive to the contractors to improving the effectiveness of their own organisation.

Nevertheless, it will be for the parties to determine for themselves how they wish to deal with this issue.

Integrated teams: secondment of personnel

One of the key features of an alliance is the creation of an integrated project team. It is also often asserted that an additional key feature is that 'the best person for the job' should be selected for each post on the project team, irrespective of which of the alliance parties that individual comes from.

While there is nothing wrong with this in principle, it is important to recognise that each of the parties to the alliance agreement does have individual corporate accountabilities (as defined by the works contracts). It is important that this is recognised and taken account of in the alliance agreement in respect of applying 'the best person for the job' concept. This will usually take the form of wording that makes it clear that the company to which any person is 'seconded' will be wholly accountable for the performance of that person insofar as he is employed in connection with discharging that company's contractual obligations.

Indemnities

Indemnities and exclusion of liability provisions between the owner and each of the other parties in the alliance agreement will be specifically covered in the relevant works contracts. However, some contractors see alliancing as an opportunity to attempt to obtain further indemnities from the owner. In particular, there is often an attempt to have the owner grant an indemnity against any claims from third parties, something which the company will usually have declined to do in works contracts except in some very special circumstances. There is nothing inherent in alliancing that should lead to a change in the company's practice in relation to indemnities.

However, it is advisable to incorporate an 'avoidance of doubt' clause in the alliance agreement, which makes it clear that the indemnity and exclusion of liability provisions in works contracts between the owner and each of the contractors also apply to property and personnel associated with the alliance agreement.

A further issue is whether or not there should be provisions in the alliance agreement whereby the alliance contractors can exchange mutual hold-harmless indemnities. Inclusion of such provision could, for example, avoid the possibility of one contractor suing another in respect of failing to achieve gainshare.

No partnership, etc.

It is probably advisable to include a clause that makes it absolutely clear that the alliance is not a partnership in the legal sense or a legal entity in its own right. However, if such a clause is to be included, legal advice should be taken as to the effectiveness of such a clause in the particular circumstances.

Release

It would be advisable to include a provision to the effect that each of the contractors 'releases and waives' its rights to receive payments under the works contracts for any items that should have been included in the final cost calculation after gainshare has been calculated and paid. This is a simple precautionary measure to prevent the possible understatement of the final cost. However, care needs to be exercised in the wording of the 'release' provisions in order to ensure that any issue outstanding at the time when gainshare is paid (e.g. insurance) is not accidentally compromised.

Confidentiality

It is a normal practice to include confidentiality provisions relating to the alliance agreement itself. However, it may also be appropriate to include wider provisions covering intellectual property and information management.

5.5.5 Other clauses

As the alliance agreement is a legal document, it will almost certainly require so-called 'boilerplate clauses' covering such issues as:

- definitions and interpretation
- term of the agreement
- assignment
- law
- waiver
- notices
- entire agreement
- intent.

6. The alliance incentive scheme

Summary

Constructing a satisfactory alliance incentive scheme is an area that can cause significant concerns, both to those new to alliancing and those who have had some experience with the concept.

General guidance and advice on the alliance incentive scheme is given in Part 2, Section 5, whereas this section provides more detailed guidance on and advice in relation to constructing the incentive scheme. Examples drawn from actual alliances are used to illustrate many of the key points and principles.

Contents

- **Definition of project completion**

- **Setting performance criteria targets**
  Capital cost
  − Owner and contractor concerns
  − Preparing the cost estimate
  − Setting the cost target
  Schedule

- **Shares in the incentive scheme**

- **Incentive scheme formulae**

- **Changes to performance criteria targets**

- **Excluded risks**

This section provides guidance on the key issues related to negotiating an alliance incentive scheme which is acceptable to all the parties in the alliance and which creates commercial alignment.

6.1 Definition of project completion

It is important to address the issue of defining project completion for the purpose of the incentive scheme at an early stage. The reason for this is that the agreed definition will have an impact on the generation of appropriate project cost estimates and implementation schedules from which the performance targets will be derived. As noted in Part 2, Section 5, it is recommended that this be defined in a way that it can be demonstrated that the project meets the key functionality requirements. It is equally important that a simple straightforward definition is used so that it can easily be determined that completion has been achieved.

The following are examples of definitions of project completion that have been used on various alliance projects.

Example 1. 'Beneficial operation' means the achievement of sustained production of the following grades and rates over a 24-hour period:

Product A	25 te/h	Design grade XX
Product B	30 te/h	Design grade YY

Example 2. 'Beneficial operation' means the achievement of sustained production from the plant for a period of 30 days without any shutdown for any technical reason, and the demonstration that the plant meets each of the criteria set out in Article 2 and Article 3 of Appendix 4 of this Alliance Agreement over a continuous period of 72 hours.

Example 3. 'Beneficial operation' means the achievement of pellet production over a continuous period of 72 hours at the following rate and grade:

C6LLDPE	25 te/h	Design grade LL6208

and when each extruder has operated at the above rates and grades for a minimum of 24 hours during the above-mentioned 72-hour period.

6.2 Setting performance criteria targets

6.2.1 Capital cost

The intent is that a project target cost is agreed between the owner and the alliance contractors against which actual cost performance will compared for the purpose of determining risk or reward payments. The performance cost target should be derived from a cost estimate which the owner will also use to determine the sum of money that it will allocate (sanctioned sum) to the project.

It is recommended that the project target cost should cover the total scope of the project, including the owner's own costs and the costs of contractors, subcontractors and suppliers not within the alliance. The rationale for this is simply that:

■ one or other of the parties in the alliance (including the owner) will be accountable for the delivery and performance of the other parties who are not in the alliance

■ the whole intent is that the alliance will be judged, and the parties to it rewarded, on the basis of the outcome of the complete project.

Owner and contractor concern

Both the owner and the contractors will have concerns about agreeing a project target cost and it is as well that all parties acknowledge that this is the case. The owner is usually concerned that he will be put into a position where the alliance members will seek to inflate the cost estimate so as to make rewards easier to achieve, and consequently that the he will be forced to accept a project cost target that he considers to be too high. Conversely, the alliance members will usually be concerned that the owner will attempt to set a project cost target that is overly ambitious and is perceived by them to be extremely difficult to achieve.

The owner's and contractors concerns can be managed in a number of ways, including establishing, *at a very early stage*:

- the principles of how the project cost target will be derived
- clear ground rules and a methodology for establishing the cost estimate.

The ground rules should include:

- A clear undertaking by the owner that it will not look to 'squeeze' contractors' 'normal profit' expectations in order to meet its aspirations for making a positive investment decision.
- Clear 'rules' that will apply in making decisions in respect of the project (e.g. if life-cycle costs are an important criterion for the owner, then he must make it clear that this will be taken into account when choosing individual items of plant, equipment, etc.).
- Any audit requirements the owner, and indeed the contractors, may have in respect of verifying and validating the cost estimate.
- Any specific requirement the owner may have with regard to validating overheads and other aspects of the cost estimate.
- Details of any external or internal benchmarking that it is intended to carry out, and how the results of such benchmarking will be handled.

It will be appropriate to deal with most of these issues as part of the selection process.

Preparing the cost estimate

To generate 'ownership' of the cost estimate and hence of the target cost, it is vitally important that it is prepared jointly by all the parties to the alliance, including the owner, and ideally on 'an open book basis'. It is recommended that:

- each of parties prepare the estimate for their own scope of work (cost data furnished as part of the selection process should be used for this purpose)
- the individual estimates are compiled into an overall project cost estimate (usually by the owner)
- the overall estimate is made available to all the parties and is subject to their review and challenge.

It is recognised that, in some instances, contractors may, for commercial confidentiality reasons, be reluctant to release their cost estimates to other contractors. If this is the case then a procedure should be agreed between the parties aimed at allowing each of them to be satisfied that the estimates prepared by the others are acceptable.

The cost estimate should be comprehensive and cover the full scope of the aspects required to achieve project completion, as defined for the purposes of the incentive scheme. It should include:

- all contractors' estimated base costs
- all contractors' profit and overhead elements
- the owner's estimated base costs
- estimated base costs of all other goods and services required to complete the scope for which the alliance is accountable.

Note: The term 'base costs' is used here to indicate costs that do not include any 'contingency' provisions. They are the 'best' estimates for undertaking the scope to which they apply. The resulting estimate is then termed the 'base estimate'.

All estimates have a range of uncertainty attached to them. This range will be influenced by a number of factors, including:

- the quality of the project definition on which the estimate is based
- the uncertainties attached to quantities and individual costs
- technical uncertainties
- design development to bring the project to its completed state
- the risks to which the project is exposed (these will include risks which are 'internal' to the project itself and external risks).

In an alliance is extremely important that all the parties fully understand the range of uncertainty attached to the cost estimate. This can best be achieved by subjecting the base cost estimate to a probabilistic risk analysis. This will enable both the overall impact of the identified uncertainties and risks to be 'scientifically' assessed, and the risks and uncertainties to be ranked in order of importance. The output from a typical cost risk analysis diagram is shown in Figure 17.

Figure 17

A typical cost probability curve

A realistic cost estimate will include an allowance to cover the uncertainties and risks. This is sometimes referred to as 'contingency', and many approaches to determining contingency are used. However, a probabilistic risk analysis also allows a suitable level of contingency to be identified in a more scientific way. One of the outputs from the risk analysis is the so-called 'expected value outcome'. This simply

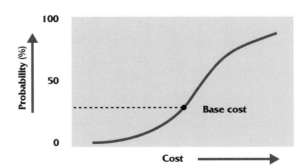

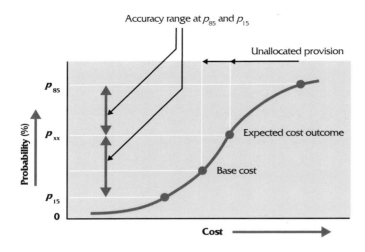

Figure 18

*Detailed output from a
cost probability curve*

represents the most likely cost of the project in statistical terms. The difference between the expected value outcome and the base estimate is usually termed the 'unallocated provision'. This represents the sum of money which on a statistical (and an historical) basis can be expected to be spent in addition to the base estimate in order to complete the project, but which cannot be allocated to specific areas of the project. In other words unallocated provision can be viewed as a project contingency. Figure 18 illustrates these points.

All the parties in the alliance should have the opportunity and be actively encouraged to contribute to the risk analysis. This not only ensures that the range of uncertainties and risks is more comprehensive, but has the added benefit of allowing all the parties to have a better understanding of the overall quality of the cost estimate.

Setting the project cost target

Having agreed a project cost estimate, the question that then has to be addressed and agreed by the parties is where on the cost probability curve the performance target cost should be set. It is at this point that tensions between the owner and the contractors are most likely to arise. The owner may well have a natural tendency to want to set the target as low on the curve as possible, with the contractors tending towards setting it as high on the curve as possible.

Referring back to the discussion above on probabilistic risk analysis, another way of expressing the expected value outcome in layman's terms is that it is equivalent to 'normal' or expected performance. Viewed like this, there is a strong argument for setting the performance target cost at, or at least close to, the expected value outcome, and this is an approach which has been adopted by many alliances. However, there have been examples of targets being set at both lower and higher levels.

Owners often seek to justify setting lower targets on the basis that it is necessary to set a 'stretch target' in order to promote performance. While this may have both a philosophical and practical basis, the wisdom of applying it contractually in an incentive scheme is less obvious. For example, having a 'low' performance target cost means that it may be viewed by contractors and project personnel as being unrealistic, or even unachievable, and if this is the case it will impact on their attitudes and, indeed, performance.

Note: Unconsidered use of terminology in respect of targets can lead to problems. Appendix 1 provides more information and distinguishes three different targets that are useful in the context of an alliance.

6.2.2 Schedule

Performance schedule targets, or targets, as may be appropriate, should be derived from a jointly prepared schedule for the project. The schedule must be consistent with the definition of project completion that has been agreed for the purpose of the incentive scheme.

Like cost estimates, schedules are also subject to risks and uncertainties, and the potential impact of these also needs to be assessed and understood by all the parties. As for the cost estimate, probabilistic risk analysis can be usefully employed in this respect.

The general principle described above for setting the target cost should also be applied in respect of setting the performance schedule target.

6.3 Shares in the incentive scheme

Many approaches to determining the share that each of the parties has in the incentive scheme have been used, and it is probably true that there is no one 'best practice' in this regard. Nevertheless, and given that the underlying principle is that there should be an equitable sharing of risk and reward, there are probably four factors that should be taken into consideration in determining the shares of the parties:

- the amount of money that contractors, both collectively and individually, are willing to put at risk
- the point at which the cap on a contractor's risk takes effect (i.e. the extent to which the target cost has to be overrun before the contractors lose all their risk money)
- whether or not the impact of the reward side has a relatively equal impact on the 'profitability' of each of the parties
- the proportion of the total savings that the owner is willing to allocate to the contractors.

Clearly these factors do not have a direct relationship, and so it will be necessary for some trading-off to occur in order to reach an outcome that is satisfactory to all the parties. From an owner's perspective, it points to the desirability of being willing to state some general principles and expectations at an early stage.

Figure 19 illustrates graphically some examples of how risks and rewards have been shared on alliances.

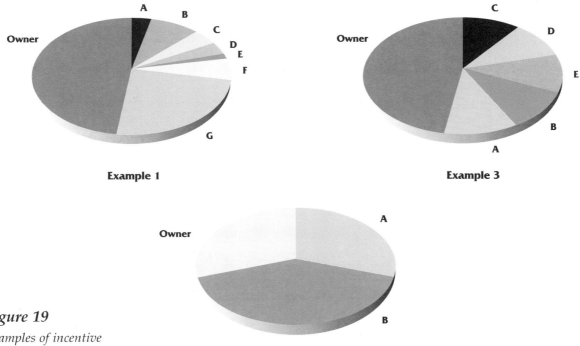

Figure 19

Examples of incentive scheme shares

6.4 Incentive scheme formulae

One specific point that is reiterated here is that each of the criteria should, ideally, be self-funding. The reasons for this can be explained as follows. Some alliances have chosen to fund rewards against both cost and schedule criteria out of savings in capital cost. In other words, a proportion of any capital-cost savings is allocated to capital-cost performance and part is allocated to schedule performance. This approach could lead to the anomalous situation that a project could be delivered exactly on the performance target cost but, say, much earlier than the performance schedule target, in which case the owner would clearly benefit but the contractors would receive no reward.

It is also recommended that there should be a formula for calculating the risk and reward payments for each of the performance criteria, and that total risk and reward payments should be determined by aggregating the results for each. Example of risk and reward formulae for a variety of criteria taken from past alliances are illustrated in Figures 20 to 22.

6.5 Changes to performance criteria targets

It is vital that the circumstances under which performance criteria targets may be changed after they have been agreed and incorporated in the alliance agreement are clear and unambiguous. It is considered to be equally important that the circumstance under which changes can occur are restrictive. There are two reasons for this:

- it provides a platform for changing the 'mindset' and attitudes of all parties towards 'claims' and the owner's attitudes towards changing the scope or functionality once execution is under way
- it will avoid replication of the costly bureaucratic processes related to 'claims' that have become a feature of many, if not the majority of, projects.

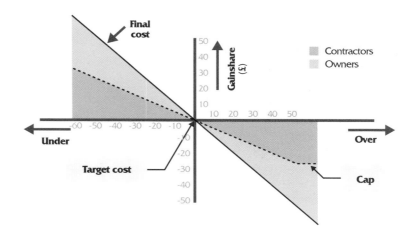

Adopting this approach is considered fundamental.

However, the acceptability of the approach is dependent on several key factors:

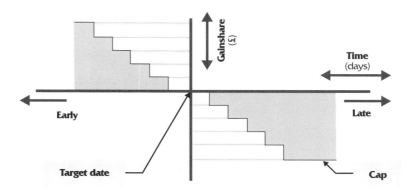

- The cost estimates and schedule must be derived from a project that is well defined and with a full understanding of the risks and uncertainties associated with it.
- The agreed target criteria must be appropriate to delivering the full scope and functionality of the project as defined at the time they are agreed.
- The target cost in particular should include appropriate allowances in the form of an

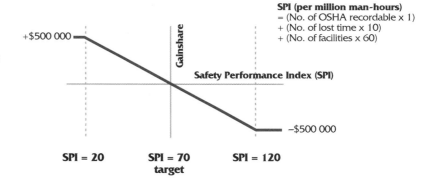

agreed level of contingency and unallocated provision to cover:
 – the design development required to complete the defined project scope and functionality
 – the risks and uncertainties associated with executing the project.

Provided these factors have been met, a device sometimes referred to as 'project intent' can be used to restrict the circumstances under which changes to the target performance criteria can take place. The basic concept is that changes to the target performance criteria can only occur if:

Figure 20 (top)
An example of a capital cost incentive scheme

Figure 21 (middle)
An example of a schedule incentive scheme

Figure 22 (bottom)
An example of a safety incentive scheme

■ there is a variation under a works contract or other contract for the supply of goods and/or services for the project

and

■ the variation is also a change to the project intent.

6.5.1 Project intent

The project intent is a brief, high-level description of the main features of the project and its intended functionality. The wording of items included in the project intent is critical, and every item should be worded such that when the question 'Has this changed or occurred?' is posed, the answer will be either 'Yes' or 'No'. There should be no ambiguity or room for interpretation. Some typical examples of project intents are given in Appendix 3.

The project intent may also be an appropriate place to incorporate 'excluded risks' (see below) against which the contractors are afforded protection.

6.5.2 'Hurdles'

In some alliance agreements 'hurdles' have also been used to further restrict changes to the target performance criteria. Hurdles operate simply by stating that, even if the other criteria for changes have been met, a change will only occur if the estimated impact on the criteria exceeds a specified value. Hurdles are designed to avoid the need to make relatively small changes. Whether there is a need for such hurdles is a moot point, as it can be argued that any change to project intent, if properly constructed, is likely to involve significant costs. In any case, the value at which the hurdle is set is a matter for negotiation.

6.5.3 *Force majeure* and suspension

Force majeure will be defined in the works contracts, as will the owner's rights to suspend a works contract. Many alliance agreements contain specific provisions as to whether or not the occurrence of *force majeure* and suspension will or will not be grounds for changing the target performance criteria. There are contrasting views on how these should or should not be grounds for making changes to the performance criteria targets, and what is acceptable in any specific project is a matter for negotiation between the parties.

6.5.4 Excluded risks

In any project there will almost always be risks which none of the parties is able to manage, mitigate or even influence. Careful consideration should be given to identifying such risks and to determining if the contractors who are party to an alliance should be afforded protection against them in respect of the incentive scheme.

A good way to start the process of reaching agreement on excluded risks is for the owner to encourage the contractors to identify risks that they consider they should be given protection against. Almost inevitably this will initially result in a relatively long list. However, experience indicates that by looking at each of the risks individually and giving careful consideration as to whether or not they are catered for in the agreed performance criteria targets cost and schedule, the final list of excluded risks is usually small.

Again it is not possible to give definitive guidance on excluded risks, as these will vary from project to project, and any case will be a subject for negotiation between the parties. However, excluded risks might include:

- changes in legislation affecting the design of the project
- proprietary or licensed technology failing to work.

The project intents given in Appendix 3 contain other examples of excluded risks.

7. Project organisation in an alliance

Summary

This section deals with two aspects of the project organisation for an alliance.

First, it deals with the design of the project team organisation and, specifically, the creation of an effective integrated team. The need to be flexible in designing the organisation and to modify it as the focus of the project changes is highlighted. Key points relating to this are illustrated using an example drawn from an alliance, and the lessons which were drawn from that in regard to making the organisation effective.

Second, the section deals with communication within the project organisation. In an alliance, effective communication assumes even greater importance than may normally be the case.

Contents

7.1 Organisational design

Some key principles that should be observed in designing project organisations for an alliance have been covered in Part 1, Section 1. These are not repeated here, but they should be considered in conjunction with this section.

The first activity that any project manager starts to think about when setting up a new project is the organisation that will be required to execute the work. Typically this is limited to considering how the resources in one's own organisation are to be marshalled and interfaced with third parties. In an alliance approach the focus needs to be on designing the total organisation across the alliance partners. This is essential if the benefits from a fully integrated team are to be realised.

All projects go through several distinct stages. These can be broadly summarised under the following headings:

- preliminary engineering and project definition
- detailed engineering and procurement
- construction
- precommissioning
- commissioning and start-up.

To be effective the project organisation will usually have to be modified to meet the changes in focus that result from moving through these different phases and to react to organisational problems as they arise. The following extended example is used to illustrate this.

7.1.1 Example

Following completion of an onshore refinery restructuring project, three distinct phases of the organisation were recognised:

(i)   statement of requirements (SOR)/FEED phase
(ii)   detailed engineering phase/first half of construction
(iii) second half of construction/commissioning and start-up phases.

During phase (i) the leading role in the technical organisation was taken by the engineering contractor and the owner's process engineering group. A high degree of integration was achieved between these teams. Project management activities, however, were focused on alliance structure and the selection of future alliance partners.

In phase (ii) the alliance agreement came into force, together with full participation of the construction alliance partners. The philosophy behind the project organisation was to have an integrated project team without duplication of functions anywhere. The organisation was built on the principle of 'best man for the job', irrespective of which alliance partner employed the person. The initial representation of the organisation was complicated, and was based on an assemblage of each alliance partner's organisation charts.

Subsequently, a different representation of the overall organisation was chosen in order to reflect better its singular functional-based nature. This representation also made it possible to express the idea of intercompany networks of teams that operated together within the overall project hierarchy. For example, procurement and cost personnel from each organisation met regularly as a team to ensure the implementation of the agreed common business processes, and to network information.

This singular organisation chart was adapted as required, and remained in use through several revisions to the end of the project. An extract from this organisation chart to show only the quality assurance and quality control functions is given in

Figure 23

An example of quality assurance and quality control organisation

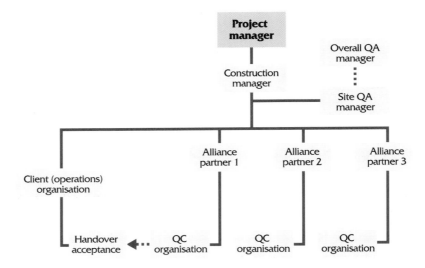

Figure 23. The organisation that was designed at this point was not tested until phase (iii), when tensions began to emerge that needed resolution.

During phase (iii) the emphasis of the project switched from engineering and procurement to construction, commissioning and start-up. Organisationally the real ground-breaking work had to be done in the field. It was here that the impact of the alliance philosophy had the greatest potential. A number of key issues had to be resolved in designing an effective construction organisation. These were:

■ The absence of main contractor discipline supervisors had to be compensated for by the construction alliance partners' own accountability for their work scopes.

■ Owner personnel who had been liaising with the refinery areas and their own technical departments during the engineering phase had to develop a different role, with the transfer of activities to site. Owner personnel took on a matrix of quality control responsibilities and enabled the final quality sign-off to be made by the owner team.

Initially, a major role was foreseen for three area superintendents who would act as area construction managers, giving leadership and taking accountability for meeting the project requirements. This was felt necessary to achieve the area-related completion and to give the necessary focus to the alliance partner organisations that were discipline based. A substantial debate was required to get the power balance correct between the area superintendents and the alliance partner project managers who took the financial accountability.

At a major construction workshop the opportunity was given to each participant to comment on the existing role descriptions, debate them with interface groups and add or negotiate missing items. The exercise was very successful and resulted in the following key changes:

- The superintendent's role was redefined to be one primarily of coordinating and problem-solving rather than one of directing the work.
- The detailed planning was reviewed in great detail by the owner and all the alliance partners and declared 'sacrosanct', and this would be used by the discipline organisation to set priorities. Superintendents would only intervene if the planning could not be followed or achieved.
- Owner role definitions were strengthened and clarified.
- Accountability for third party activities (e.g. supply and erect vendors) was better defined.

Lessons learned from the project

A number of lessons can be extracted from the above example that have general applicability and should be taken into account by those with responsibility for designing alliance project team organisations:

- Building an effective integrated organisation requires effort, with monitoring of its effectiveness on a continuing basis and a willingness to adapt to meet changing circumstances and to overcome problems that emerge.
- At the interfaces, flexible people are required who are able and willing to be 'bridges' between different cultures.
- It should be recognised that an individual's conception of what a task is (e.g. planning or cost control) is conditioned by what it means within the context of their own organisation.
- Representing an organisation on paper is not sufficient to make it operate as intended. Specific efforts need to be made to communicate intent to the team.
- The use of a workshops to receive feedback and to review the organisation that had been conceived by the management and of the individual roles within it can be an invaluable tool in identifying changes that will improve the effectiveness of the project team.
- Realism needs to be maintained around roles.

Organisations often may not have many candidates who are willing to take on the substantially wider roles that may be required of them in an alliance. Those who are willing need encouragement, support and acknowledgement from the project management team.

7.2 Communication

7.2.1 General

No matter how well thought out the project organisation is, its ability to operate effectively will depend on the communication that takes place from the project leadership to the team and within the team. The project management team needs to think explicitly about the forms of communication and the systems that are required to make it effective. This will depend on the extent of co-location of the different teams. The more geographically dispersed different parts of the organisation are, the more effort is required to ensure that consistent communications are disseminated as quickly and efficiently as possible.

7.2.2 Communication systems

Use of information technology (IT), in particular e-mail systems, is taken for granted now in most organisations. When linking up different organisations it is well worth the effort to consider an integrated IT plan to define how the most efficient connectivity can be achieved between different offices, suppliers, fabrication and construction sites. Efficient connectivity can provide an advantage in terms of ensuring reliability, consistency and security of information that far outweighs the initial costs of paying for dedicated project facilities, especially for major projects.

If new IT systems need to be installed the time and energy required for this should not be underestimated. Solutions to the technical problems involved are usually either available or can be readily found. However, it takes time for people to become familiar with the new tools and the working methods they imply. Systems should be designed to match preferred working practices, not the other way around.

7.2.3 Communication channels

Briefing sessions

The use of briefing sessions to get a consistent message to the project teams is extremely important and will require the project leadership to be active and visible in this regard. The content of briefing sessions will change over time as the organisation develops. Early in the project a major theme needs to be explanation of alliancing principles and the joint targets that have been agreed to. Briefing sessions are good forums for reviewing project status and acknowledging successes and achievements, as well as the place to articulate future challenges and requests. During the construction phase topics can focus on safety performance and related messages. To keep the sessions dynamic, video material and/or slides can be used.

Project publications

The publication of a project bulletin with news, status and topics such as interviews with staff and opinion surveys on the project performance can help generate a feeling of common purpose. Safety needs to be a recurrent theme.

Project notice boards

Extensive use can be made of project notice boards. Ensuring that the same information is issued to all notice board locations on a regular basis keeps consistency in the message. Regular updates of information confirm to the team that the project is alive and dynamic, and through the feedback given they can see the effect of actions taken to improve performance.

Workshops

Alliance organisations typically make extensive use of workshops to generate alignment in the team through the identification and debate of issues. However, a significant proportion of time needs to be dedicated to generating the shared understanding around the what, why and when of the project, before tackling issues to make workshops effective. This is part of the communication task of the management team.

Progress video

Use of video to record the progress on the project and to communicate the goals is also a good vehicle for generating a shared understanding of what the project is all about.

Project surveys

Surveys can be used to test the effectiveness of the communication programme. Questionnaires about the usefulness of, for example, briefing sessions and workshops, in the sense of what worked well and what did not, can help the management team fine tune subsequent sessions. Attitude surveys are also useful to test the way in which announced goals are perceived by the team. For example, a survey could ask the team about the confidence level they had that a particular goal would be achieved.

8. Project procedures and processes in an alliance

Summary

Each contracting party in a construction project will usually have its own set of tried and trusted procedures and processes for implementing and managing project activities.

This short section provides guidance on the creation of common procedures and processes that will apply across all the alliance members. It also shows how these can build on and be integrated with the procedures and processes of the individual members, and thus provide a complete and coherent set of processes and procedures for the alliance.

Contents

*   **Execution procedures**
*   **Reporting systems**

In an alliance there should always be an open debate about the procedures and systems that should be used for managing the project. However, experience on alliances indicates that the most successful approach is probably one where:

■   the systems of each alliance partner are used to the maximum possible extent for the execution and control of their own work
■   there is a set of common procedures that apply at the alliance level.

The common procedures should be focused on areas that apply to all the parties and where significant benefits could be realised from a unified approach. Such areas are likely to include:

Figure 24

Project quality procedures

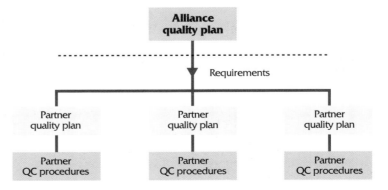

- cost control
- planning
- procurement (if more than one member is engaged in this activity).

In developing and agreeing project procedures, especially those that will be common to all parties, there needs to be a true willingness to select systems on a 'best for the job' basis and to avoid parochial protectionism.

In all cases it is recommended that a procedures document is produced that defines the scope and detail of common procedures and the minimum contents of the alliance-partner-specific procedures required, in order to ensure that project requirements are properly addressed, effective controls are implemented and the overall aims of the project are met.

8.1 Execution procedures

An approach used successfully on many alliance projects has been to develop a high-level set of plans and procedures that make up the alliance project procedure manual. This sets the requirements for lower level procedures and gives guidance to the alliance-partner-level project-specific plans. Care should be taken to ensure that there is duplication between the documents. This approach allows the maximum use of existing procedures where these do not deviate from the overall project requirements. Figure 24 shows this schematically, in this instance in respect of the alliance quality plan.

8.2 Reporting systems

The philosophy described above for execution procedures can also be used for reporting requirements, covering areas such as costs and progress. For example, cost reporting typically requires a multilevel system, with the level of detail progressively increasing from the top level to the bottom. This is required to ensure that the necessary information is captured and presented in different forms and levels of detail that are relevant to the specific user or recipient.

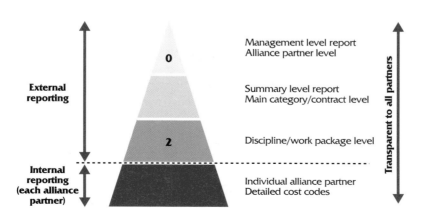

Figure 25

The cost reporting hierarchy

The same considerations apply equally in an alliance project, and there should be no need for each member company to change the way it does things. However, it is essential to define the reporting approach and the interfaces and integration of information that will be maintained. Figure 25 illustrates the various levels of cost reports that are likely to be required in an alliance.

9. Building and sustaining alliance relationships

Summary

This section provides guidance on building and sustaining effective relationships at all levels in the alliance member companies and in the integrated project management team. The main mechanism through which effective relationships are built is alignment.

The section starts with some general advice on building relationships, and then goes on to cover the importance of alignment in more detail, identifying key levels where alignment is particularly important and why that is so.

A variety of processes and mechanisms that can be employed to generate alignment are then listed, followed by examples of their use drawn from actual alliances.

This is followed by a discussion on the value of using external consultants, which has been reported by many alliances.

The section concludes with some guidance on actions geared to encouraging performance improvement and innovation, which is largely viewed as being a relationship issue.

Contents

- General principles

- The importance of alignment

- Alignment mechanisms

- Facilitation training and coaching: consultants

- Generating performance improvement and innovation

The success of alliance projects is fundamentally dependent on the relationships formed between the different parties, both at the corporate level and within the alliance project teams. Meaningful performance improvements will only be achieved if relationships are such as to permit individuals to utilise the possibilities that the alliance contract form opens up. This requires relationships to be built horizontally and vertically throughout the project organisation, in order to overcome the limitations imposed by a traditional transaction-based execution environment.

Building relationships takes time, and relationships are likely to be deepened and strengthened as a project moves through its various stages. This will only happen,

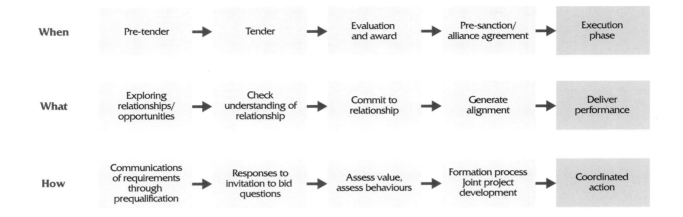

When	Pre-tender	→	Tender	→	Evaluation and award	→	Pre-sanction/ alliance agreement	→	Execution phase
What	Exploring relationships/ opportunities	→	Check understanding of relationship	→	Commit to relationship	→	Generate alignment	→	Deliver performance
How	Communications of requirements through prequalification	→	Responses to invitation to bid questions	→	Assess value, assess behaviours	→	Formation process Joint project development	→	Coordinated action

Figure 26

The development of alliance relationships

however, if there is a clear understanding of the importance of relationships and a consequent focus on relationship building. Figure 26 illustrates the various stages of an alliance and provides an overview of the focus of relationships at the various stages.

As Figure 26 indicates, relationship building should start at the earliest stages, in the prequalification documents, and subsequently the ground rules or general principles for the proposed relationship should be laid down in the initial tender documents. Further development of understanding of the relationships required and of the principles will be developed during the tender (alliance partner) selection process. However, the major effort in building the relationships will occur during the presanction period, through the opportunities afforded by:

■ having personnel from the various members working together to develop and define the project
■ the negotiation of the alliance agreement.

The real work in agreeing the principles of the relationship takes place during the negotiation of the alliance agreement. The process of each party providing input to an initial proposal, and the cycles of debate and reflection that follow will permit full ownership to develop for the agreement contents. The alliance agreement must capture the principles of the relationship developed up to the point of contract signing and the start of the formal alliance. By this point all parties need to understand and be clear about what they want the relationship to be and what they want it to achieve, even if the exact means of achievement are not yet known.

The final plank of relationship development at this stage is the communication and diffusion of the agreed principles and project goals throughout the project team. This can be most effectively achieved by direct communication from the project leadership (the owner's project team, the owner's business unit (final owner) and the contractors) to the different teams working on the project. A direct approach, with project leadership accessing personnel directly, is considered best to ensure that a consistent message is communicated to the different levels in the organisation.

Relying on information cascading down the organisation through different levels of supervision is likely to result in too much dilution and distortion of the key messages.

The main efforts during the execution phase should be directed towards nurturing, sustaining and supporting the relationships built during the earlier stages. As the project proceeds from design through to construction and commissioning, the communication efforts need to ensure that the changing mix of personnel has the same opportunity to gain a first-hand understanding of the project aims and be aligned and committed to them.

At all stages it is important to appreciate that initial enthusiasm can be significantly dampened when difficulties arise on a project, and these will test the depth of the relationships established. It is essential to prevent the parties from falling back into their old ways when difficulties appear and senior project managers (especially the owner's) will have to demonstrate their leadership and depth of commitment in the face of such difficulties.

9.1 The importance of alignment

Alignment is a prerequisite for truly coordinated action, both within an organisation and between the members of the different organisations cooperating to realise common project goals, and is of crucial importance when considering alliancing. If alignment exists, then the commitment that is equally important will almost invariably follow.

Alignment should not be confused with agreement on everything, but be viewed as the acceptance by all parties of the validity of the prescribed project outcomes and of the means chosen to achieve them. Neither should it be considered that alignment is something that, once created, will continue to exist. Steps need to be taken on a continuing basis to ensure that alignment is both maintained and reinforced.

The generation of alignment needs to be achieved at the following three distinct levels within the alliance:

- contractors' and owner's corporate level management
- contractors' and owner's project management teams
- at the working levels within the alliance project team, particularly among those at interface levels between the different alliance members.

Alignment at these levels is essential for a number of important reasons:

- Because of the mutual dependency in delivering good results for their companies, the corporate managers need to have the confidence that they can rely on each other to take actions appropriate to achieving these results.

■ Employees of a company are likely to exhibit behaviours that they perceive will be rewarded by management or that they think the management in general, but more especially their immediate managers, want to see. Mangers who are aligned and committed to the alliancing approach are more likely to want their subordinates to display the sort of behaviours that are consistent with achieving the aims of the alliance. Provided that they take steps to make this visible and their expectations known to their employees, it is more likely that employees will be prepared to make any necessary changes in their behaviours and attitudes. Thus corporate managers will have a strong influence on the project manager, who in turn will influence their discipline mangers, and so on down to the lowest levels of the project organisation.

■ The behaviours and attitudes at the interface levels will have a strong impact on the effective working of the project team. This is the level where steering forces from above start to become weaker and individuals may not be readily willing to adopt a different approach. For example, an owner's engineer may prefer to stay in a traditional superordinate role of directing, checking and controlling work, rather than be a team member that has to justify his decisions in a much wider community.

9.2 Alignment mechanisms

There are numerous process and mechanisms that can be exploited in the quest to create alignment. Some of these are given below, followed by examples drawn from actual alliances.

■ Exploit the opportunities that the alliance partner selection process and the alliance formation phase leading up to final approval for the project offer for creating alignment.

■ Have corporate level managers either lead (preferred) or be directly involved in negotiating the details of the alliance agreement. This can be a powerful mechanism for generating alignment at this level. The design of the financial incentive scheme and the development and agreement of the 'principles' being areas that are particularly valuable in this respect.

■ Use the financial incentive scheme as a vehicle for promoting alignment within the project team. Dissemination and effective communication of the details of the scheme within the project will help persuade individuals that it is in their company's and their own interest to be aligned and committed to the overall aims of the project.

■ Personnel from the different alliance member organisations working together to develop joint execution strategies, cost estimates and schedules is a powerful alignment mechanism in itself, and generates collective and individual ownership of these items.

■ Use every opportunity in the alliance formation phase to create *ad hoc* subteams to deal with specific issues and have these subteams populated by a cross-section of personnel from the member companies.

- Use extensive and intensive communications to keep personnel fully aware of all aspects of the project as a means of generating shared understanding.
- Conduct attitude surveys within the team as a means of determining actions appropriate to creating and/or maintaining alignment.
- Promote the development of mutual and intergroup debates on, for example, specific issues facing the project.
- Use an organisational design that promotes integration and alignment. One way of doing this is to construct interorganisational teams that are functionally based.
- Use facilitated workshops aimed at promoting alignment.
- Use consultants who have specific expertise in creating alignment in teams as a route to high performance.
- Arrange social events to help break down the cultural barriers that may exist between employees of the alliance member companies.

9.2.1 Examples of actions to create alignment

Example 1

Prior to issuing the tender documents for the role of engineer, the owner invited all preselected bidders to an informal get together and dinner. The following morning he gave a briefing session on alliancing. The assembled chief executive officers were invited to express their views on an the alliance approach and their commitment to the project.

Example 2

In an alliance where all the alliance partners were engaged in procurement, a purchasing team was formed that comprised the lead purchasing personnel from each partner. This functional steering committee agreed the common processes that would be applied to the procurement activities. The process of jointly reaching these agreements helped generate the alignment sought at the working level. Prior to this taking place, however, the requirement for common procurement practices had to be initiated by the project management team.

Example 3

An attitude survey was carried out among the managers, supervisors and other employees of all five alliance members towards the end of a successful alliance project. The following were noted:

- managers in all companies were the most enthusiastic participants (above supervisors and others)
- all levels of construction company respondents showed high levels of enthusiasm
- lower levels of enthusiasm were shown by owner and engineering contractors, supervisors and others.

These results were interpreted as being illustrative of the degree to which the empowerment of particular groups and individuals increased or decreased depending on the phase of the job and their role in it.

Example 4

A workshop was held immediately after alliance formation and was attended by corporate and project management personnel. They exchanged views around the following questions:

- What is in it for me?
- What am I good at?
- What do I bring to this project?
- What can the other alliance partners count on me for?
- What single request do you have of other alliance partners to ensure the success of the project?

Participants reported that the workshop had helped them develop a level of appreciation and understanding of others that greatly facilitated the development of the joint and coordinated action in the remainder of the project.

Example 5

One alliance held a 2-day workshop 3 weeks after final project approval (sanction). The objective of the workshop was to develop project team commitments for the execution phase of the project. A group of 60 people representing all the member companies attended. Consultants led the workshop.

By the end of the workshop the group had jointly developed, agreed and signed a 'commitment statement', which incorporated the targets that the team had agreed on as well as other points relating to the alliance relationship. At the highest level the team's, targets were directly related to the performance criteria targets (cost and schedule) embodied in the financial incentive scheme of the alliance agreement. The targets that were set for these exceeded the targets in the alliance agreement.

The team then used the targets in their day-to-day management of the project as 'stretch targets'. The commitment statement became an important management tool for maintaining project relationships. For example, new people joining the project were invited to sign up to the commitments made by the original group. This invitation was nearly always enthusiastically received.

The ownership of these ambitious targets stimulated the team in a constant search for ways of achieving them, and was regarded a being a major contributing factor to the eventual successful outcome of the project.

Example 6

'Canteen' sessions were held for home office and construction staff at regular intervals for all team members (this meant all companies, whether alliance partners or not) and all employees. The initial purpose was to inform the attendees of the project goals and the special alliance approach, while subsequently the main purpose was to give feedback on performance directly to the workforce. The investment in time, although significant, was considered well worthwhile to ensure that the whole workforce remained aligned and committed to the project, irrespective of which company it worked for.

9.3 Facilitation, training and coaching: consultants

Several references have been made to the potential value of using facilitation and high performance team building consultants in the process of building and sustaining relationships. This raises the question as to whether the use of such consultants is a prerequisite for the success of an alliance. The majority of successful alliances (and indeed other forms of partnering) have clearly indicated their belief that the benefits they derived from utilising these techniques was a key factor in that success of the projects, even though not all of them used external consultants.

Example. One small-scale survey of nine alliance projects showed that of these five used external facilitators and four did not. Of the five projects that used consultants, all respondents confirmed that they had been effective in aligning behaviours.

So, while it is not possible to state categorically that external consultants should be utilised, there is a number of reasons why their use should be seriously considered:

- They can more readily introduce a common language into the project team (which consists of several companies each with their own culture). This helps to define a project culture that is distinct from any of the individual company cultures. Jointly defining common terminology also generates common understanding of the purpose, goals, targets and *raison d'être* of the alliance itself.
- It is difficult for any one of the project managers to be discharging their operational responsibility one day and leading a team-building type session the next. The required styles are rather different and will introduce role conflict in the individual, and confusing messages may be given to the project team.
- One of the project managers attempting to facilitate multiparty sessions will not be seen as impartial or neutral in their actions, however close they may be to impartiality. A consultant can bring this impartiality.
- Consultants can help project leaders see and acknowledge their own shortcomings and weaknesses.
- Consultants are more likely to accelerate the alignment and integration of the team. Speed of integration is crucial if performance improvements are to be realised within the relatively short lifetime of a single project.

While consultants are seen as a positive factor in developing alliances, it must never be forgotten that they are not an executing party, and maturity must be maintained around their role. They do not, and should not be allowed to, make decisions, particularly decisions related to the implementation of the project. They help people come to the right decisions themselves.

The training and coaching of individuals is of particular relevance in partnerships, since many people are going to be expected to step out of their traditional roles and are going to be asked to form working-level links with members of other organisations. Issues such as responsibility and authority will become blurred for some.

Coaching of individuals will be a role for senior management, who will also need to lead by example. Here, again, consultants working with the project team can play an important role in identifying coaching needs and assisting in coaching.

9.4 Generating performance improvement and innovation

The whole purpose of an alliance is to improve performance in all areas of the project with a view to bettering the agreed target performance criteria embedded in the alliance agreement. This subsection provides some guidance on how performance improvements may be achieved.

Generating performance improvement in all areas is highly dependent on encouraging innovation and on the willingness to challenge established solutions at both the technical and the business process level. It is important to foster an environment where there will be no blame for good ideas that do not work, in order not to stifle further desire to improve among the team for fear of retribution. The project management team must also carefully balance the need for innovation against the very real need to deliver the project on time. Some good ideas will inevitably have to be acknowledged as being too late to be incorporated or as too untested for use at a particular stage of the project.

To stimulate and record engineering innovations it is recommended that a channel for improvement ideas is provided. This is best done by means of a formal procedure that encourages individuals, and preferably groups of individuals, formally to submit good ideas for cost savings to the project management team for approval. It is important that:

■ Each idea for improvement is properly assessed to establish that the full consequences of implementing it are understood before deciding to adopt it. This will mitigate against adopting ideas that could threaten the overall objectives of the project, and ensure that any safety, quality or operability implications for the owner are not going to be missed.

■ All decisions to implement any idea are documented and recorded, particularly where they represent a departure from established specifications.

10. Monitoring performance in an alliance

Summary

This short section focuses on specific issues relating to performance monitoring in an alliance and is not intended to provide a detailed guide to monitoring and reporting systems *per se*.

Emphasis is placed on the need to create and maintain clarity around the terminology used to describe the various types of targets that will usually exist within an alliance and on how reporting against these will be accomplished.

Approaches to and techniques that can be used to monitor the quality of relationships are identified, and an example of relationship quality monitoring is given.

Contents

- Performance against incentive-scheme targets
  Capital cost and schedule
- Safety performance
- Relationship quality

The purpose of this section is simply to highlight some key issues in respect of monitoring performance that are of particular relevance in an alliance. It is not intended to provide a detailed guide to the monitoring and reporting systems that are an essential part of any well-managed project. From this perspective there are two issues that need to be focused on:

- performance against the target criteria that are used in the alliance agreement financial incentive scheme
- the quality of the relationships.

10.1 Performance against incentive-scheme targets

If corrective actions are to be effective, monitoring performance in an open-book reimbursable environment requires a special emphasis on forecasting rather than on reporting. Clarity around targets and what constitutes good performance is also essential. For example, the cost reporting system may indicate that an individual party is exceeding their allocated budget. However, there may simply have been an underestimate of the quantity of work to be performed, and in reality their performance may actually be good.

Care needs to be taken to examine and investigate all cases where performance appears poor in order to check whether or not this really is the case. This will assist in avoiding tensions between the companies, which could undermine the relationships and unity of purpose. More importantly, if performance really is poor, then such investigations can lead to identifying the reasons for this and developing solutions to overcome them.

Sometimes serious misunderstandings can occur within companies due to a lack of clarity around project reports. This can especially be an issue where the project team has set its own delivery or 'stretch' targets for the execution phase which are quite different from those embodied in the financial incentive scheme. Having set such targets, the project team will naturally want to know at any point in time how well they are performing against them and report that performance. However, responsible corporate reporting requires a more prudent approach, with reporting being done against the cost estimates, project schedules, etc., that formed the basis of the owner's approval to proceed. These different targets are discussed in more detail in Appendix 2.

The importance of keeping a clear distinction about the issue of the delivery targets of a project is illustrated by the following example.

Example. One large offshore project in Norway came in for public criticism because of a perceived overrun in costs. In reality, the project was a great success because it was actually delivered at costs that were substantially below those that could have been expected based on historical cost data. The public perception that the project was a failure was because the actual costs were somewhat above the extremely ambitious stretch targets that had been set and, more importantly, which had received considerable and unqualified publicity in the media.

Figure 27

An example of alliance cost reporting

One approach to surmounting this issue is to monitor and report progress and produce an outcome forecast against both sets of targets. The key to successful implementation of this type of approach is to ensure that it is fully understood by corporate managers, including board members, as appropriate.

This approach is shown graphically in Figure 27. The cost development history shows that the project team forecast an underrun in the project cost of X at the 30% project completion stage. However, only Y was formally

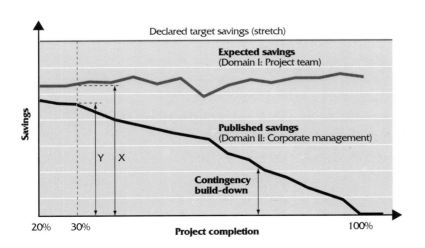

reported to corporate management at this point, in order to take account of uncertainty in the future elements of the project execution. Fortunately, in this case X was almost realised, and was reported in a phased manner to corporate management through to project completion.

If it is intended to operate such an approach it is recommended that a procedure governing its operation be developed before reporting starts. The procedure should be based on good project management practices and should include an agreed contingency build-down. The principles outlined here can be adapted for application in monitoring incentive scheme schedules targets.

10.2 Safety performance

The conventional approach to safety performance measurement is output based recording of statistics for near misses, incidents and injuries. The alliance environment is conducive to developing proactive safety programmes, accessing the entire construction workforce in the same way with the same message.

A comprehensive safety programme will comprise many initiatives that have become commonplace on modern construction sites, such as toolbox meetings, unsafe behaviour observation rounds, personal protective gear checks, and monitoring housekeeping standards to name some of the more common ones. These can all be used to serve as input monitors that can be correlated with safety performance. For example, if most project and construction managers believe that a clean site is a safe site, then scoring general housekeeping on a weekly basis gives advance warning of potential problems, and further regular scoring enables improvements or deterioration to be monitored and corrective action taken.

Example. One alliance project established a safety incentive programme by scoring a large number of parameters each week. When a predetermined level of points was reached, the entire workforce received a safety gift of nominal value. The programme was a successful way of keeping safety visible and on the agenda at all times. The programme could be referred to in workplace meetings and issues addressed. Reward was collective and all parties had to contribute to get satisfactory results. Equally, poor safety performance did not result in punishment or withdrawal of reward, but merely in a delay until the next milestone was reached.

10.3 Relationship quality

While the clear and accurate monitoring and reporting of tangible results such as cost, schedule and safety are essential, the success of alliance projects ultimately depends on the relationships that are formed within and between the different teams contributing to the project. Consequently, measuring the performance of the project relationship can be a valuable tool in generating this awareness and in giving feedback to the management team on how well the alliance is developing.

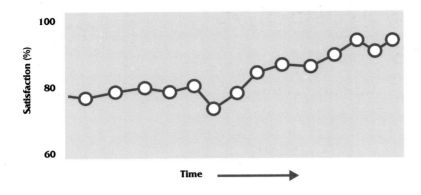

Satisfaction (%)

100

80

60

Time

Figure 28

An example of relationship evaluation over time

Techniques that can give some insight into relationship performance include:

■ attitude surveys among the project team
■ meeting effectiveness surveys
■ major event *post mortems* (e.g. after a major shutdown or other critical activity)
■ evaluation of crisis resolution efforts.

Regular application of attitude surveys can be particularly valuable in revealing trends, which can highlight specific issues that may need to be the subject of special attention. In instituting such measures it is recommended that serious consideration be given to engaging external assistance.

Example. On a recent alliance, a regular (monthly) evaluation against ten criteria was instituted to assess the relationship between the main site representatives of the owner and contractor. The project involved work in an existing facility which continued to operate while project work was in progress. The criteria included items such as:

■ interference with the operation of the existing facility
■ flexibility to meet changing demands
■ response to and resolution of problems.

The overall results of the evaluation over more than a year are depicted graphically in Figure 28. The results were used on a monthly basis to identify and resolve problem areas and to monitor the state of the relationship over a longer term. As can be seen, the general trend with time was that the relationship was improving. The owner reported that the significant dips were directly related to work requiring the existing plant to be shut down and to the stresses which that raised.

Further details on approaches to monitoring and measuring as well as specific examples of their application are given in Section 2.5 of the ECI publication *Partnering in the Public Sector*.

11. Building relationships with others

Summary

This section covers the important topic of building effective relationships with companies, organisations and individuals who are not members of the alliance but who nevertheless can have a profound impact on whether or not the alliance will meet its objectives.

The major part of the section deals with companies and organisations that will be directly supplying goods and services to the project – the so-called 'procurement chain'. The importance of these companies to the results obtained on a project is discussed, and a variety of approaches to making their contribution more effective is described and discussed.

A proactive approach to developing relationships with government and local authorities and with other external organisations and individuals is recommended.

Contents

- **Non-alliance companies**
  The procurement chain
  – Overall importance
  – Procurement chain relationships
  – The procurement chain: supply and demand
  – Timing of involvement
  – Building effective relationships
  Strategy
  Communicating the intent of the alliance
  Open dialogue
  Commercial considerations
  Integration
  Communication

- **Relationships with external authorities**

- **Relationships with other external organisations and individuals**

No matter how well aligned and committed the members of the alliance are, there are others who can influence the ability of the alliance to deliver its objectives and fulfil its potential. These others fall into three categories:

■ Companies and organisations in the procurement chain (i.e. subcontractors, vendors and suppliers directly providing specific goods and services to and for the project). These are referred to in this book as 'non-alliance companies'.

■ Government, local and statutory authorities that have a direct involvement in the project.

■ External organisations and individuals not directly involved in the project but who have or may take an interest in it (e.g. the press, pressure groups, both formal and informal, and local communities).

For an alliance to have the maximum opportunity to achieve its aims, it is necessary for it to put in place appropriate processes to both build and manage relationships with these external bodies.

11.1 Non-alliance companies

11.1.1 The procurement chain

Overall importance

The criticality of the alliance members' relationships with non-alliance companies in the procurement chain can initially be judged by the fact that the goods and services they provide usually account for a significant proportion (typically 30–60%) of the total cost of the project. However, the direct cost of procured goods and services is not the only factor that matters. The performance of companies in the procurement chain will also have a direct impact on the project implementation schedule. Failure of an individual subcontractor or supplier to deliver at the right time can have an impact far beyond the direct costs of its goods or services. In addition, of course, the performance of each individual company in the procurement chain will impact on the overall quality of the completed project, and may impact also on safety performance.

The non-alliance companies can also impact, for good or bad, on the ability of the alliance to be flexible in reacting to and dealing with changes that occur. Moreover, they can help to resolve issues that arise in ways that are effective in terms of cost, time and quality.

These factors need to be carefully considered and weighed in selecting non-alliance companies and in constructing effective relationships with them. The specific value that can be derived from improved relationships with the procurement chain are illustrated by the following example.

Example. On two large North Sea projects major equipment and material were obtained at a direct cost some 30% (about £20 million) less than had been budgeted for.

Procurement chain relationships in an alliance

The procurement chain relationships are perhaps best looked at as consisting of three main tiers below the owner, with those contractors or suppliers who are not members of the alliance comprising the second and third tiers. The contractual relationships between alliance members and the second- and third-tier non-alliance companies can, and usually will, take different forms.

The choice lies between:

- so-called suballiances, or vertical alliances, between an alliance member and a group of non-alliance companies from the second and third tiers

■ direct one-to-one relationships between an alliance member and individual non-alliance companies.

The choice of which route to go will depend on a number of factors related to the non-alliance companies:

■ their size
■ the nature of the goods and/or services they will provide
■ the criticality of their goods and services to the project
■ the importance of their interfaces with the design process
■ the importance of the project to their business
■ their commercial and contractual attitudes to conducting business
■ existing relationships they may have with alliance members.

One of the alliance members (whether it be the owner or one of the alliance members) may well already have well-established relationships with non-alliance companies which the parties to the alliance agree will be of benefit to meeting the alliance objectives. For example, the owner may have 'framework' agreements in place for various items of materials and/or equipment supply. Such relationships ought to be taken into account when developing the strategy for selecting non-alliance companies.

Figure 29

Relationships between the alliance and the supply chain

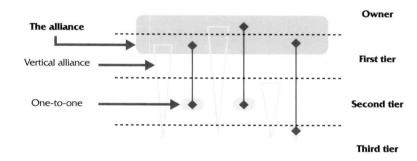

The different types of relationships within the procurement chain are illustrated in Figure 29.

The procurement chain: supply and demand

Any procurement chain has two principal aspects: the demand chain and the supply chain. The procurement chain that is initiated and evolves from the alliance members is the demand chain, where the demand that is specified by and originates from the alliance has to be fulfilled by and supplied from the second- and third-tier non-alliance companies. These aspects of the procurement chain are illustrated in Figure 30.

Figure 30

Procurement demand and supply chains

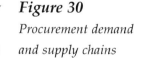
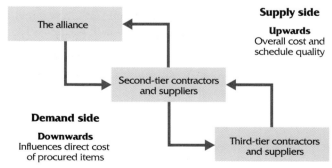

Distinguishing between the demand and supply aspects is important because:

■ the alliance members (the demand chain) have a significant impact on cost because they specify what the demand is

■ the quality of the response of the supply chain to these 'demands' has a direct impact on the project implementation schedules and the quality of the project.

11.1.2 Timing of involvement

Figure 31

The timing of supply chain involvement

As with the alliance members, the timing of involvement of non-alliance companies can influence the overall results. Figure 31 gives some illustrative guidance on the timing of involvement. Irrespective of whether potential chain companies are directly involved at an early stage, early dialogue with them can be beneficial.

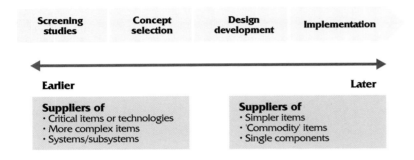

Example. One alliance reported that, through dialogue with suppliers, it was found possible to delay placement of orders until later than usual and when design was further advanced. The effect was reduced changes due to design alterations.

11.2 Building effective relationships

The overriding aim of the alliance must be to obtain the best possible alignment with the non-alliance companies in the procurement. The better or more complete this alignment is the more likely it is that the overall objectives of the alliance will be achieved. Given the diversity of the companies in the supply chain, there is unlikely to be a single unique recipe or formula that can be applied across the board to achieve alignment. Neither would this necessarily be desirable, because it would imply a degree of imposition which, experience shows, is not a good way of building effective relationships. Nevertheless, it can equally be asserted that the general principles, which apply to achieving alignment between the alliance members themselves, apply here as well. Some practical measures aimed at building effective relationships through the procurement chain are discussed in more detail below.

11.2.1 Strategy

The alliance should develop at an early stage an overall strategy for engaging with potential non-alliance contractors, selecting non-alliance companies and building relationships with them. A detailed plan to implement the strategy should also be developed. Among other things, the strategy should address the diversity issues discussed above, and be tailored to take account of them. At the same time it should allow for flexibility of approach.

For example, it will almost always be sensible to group potential non-alliance companies in accordance with the criticality of the goods or services to be provided and/or the importance of their interfaces with the design process. This will enable limited alliance resources to be better utilised through greater concentration on key areas, and bring greater focus to issues such as creating a commercial mechanism that is aligned to meeting overall objectives.

11.2.2 Communicating the intent of the alliance

The non-alliance companies need to be given a full and proper understanding of:

- the objectives of the project
- how it is being/will be organised and run
- how each of the non-alliance companies fits in
- how their contribution and involvement affects and interacts with others.

Without this, it is unlikely that they will be able to maximise the effectiveness of their contribution to the project. Developing the non-alliance companies' understanding can, and should, be part of the process of selecting them. However, there is a case for starting this at an even earlier stage.

Example. Many alliances have organised briefing sessions for potential suppliers of goods and services before staring the selection processes. These sessions can be arranged around specific products or services, or around groups of products or services, depending on the importance and/or criticality of the products and services involved. At these sessions the project team provides all relevant project background information as well as detailed information relevant to the potential participation of the non-alliance companies. The project team has also used these sessions as an opportunity to articulate any specific principles that it would like to apply in conducting business with the non-alliance companies, and to emphasise their recognition that the non-alliance companies are vital contributors to the success or otherwise of the project.

11.2.3 Open dialogue

Effective and productive relationships rarely develop when one of the parties adopts a dictatorial or 'prescriptive' approach, whether it be in respect of delivery schedule, contractual terms and conditions, form of remuneration, or other matters. The same is true with respect to relationships with non-alliance contractors.

A genuinely open dialogue with potential procurement chain companies should take place with as few preconditions attached as possible. The approach by the alliance members will be critical in this regard. While they need to be clear about what they believe is required to meet the project objectives, they also need to be willing to listen to the point of view of the procurement chain companies. Alliance members should always:

- remember that the vendor must complete a design–procure–manufacture cycle
- remember that the vendor will have other commitments to fulfil
- ask themselves, and indeed the vendor, what they can do to help the vendor to deliver
- remember that the direct costs of the vendor might not be the most critical factor in achieving the overall objectives.

11.2.4 Commercial considerations

Care should be taken to avoid trying to apply or impose specific remuneration terms on vendors and suppliers. At first sight it may appear that adopting a financial incentive scheme to mirror that which applies to the alliance is desirable, and in many cases this may indeed be true. However, it will certainly not be appropriate in all cases, and the alliance members need to be willing to take a balanced and mature view after taking full account of the views of the non-alliance company.

11.2.5 Integration

Many of the non-alliance companies have to provide data and/or services that are critical to the effective and timely execution of the design. Depending on the criticality of the data and the complexity of the interfaces, there may be significant gains to be made by integrating or co-locating non-alliance personnel with the project team, even if this is for relatively short periods at critical times.

11.2.6 Communication

Non-alliance companies are unlikely to meet the needs of the project and maximise their contribution unless they are kept aware of all relevant information. In the past, relationships with suppliers of goods and services tended to be on a relatively arms-length basis, with the information given to suppliers by the owner or main contractor organisation being restricted. Equally, there are many examples of changes having occurred in the project circumstances and which were important to the suppliers, but where the information was not communicated to them. On the other hand, there are also many past examples of owner and main contractor organisations suffering from the failure of their suppliers to keep them informed of changes, delays, etc.

All of this must be changed if the performance of the procurement chain is to be maximised. The alliance members (particularly the owner) must take a lead in encouraging the exchange of all relevant information on a continuing basis. It is extremely important to make it clear that being made aware of 'bad' as well as 'good' news is considered to be valuable, as this will give the alliance a much better chance of responding in a meaningful and effective way. A vital part of achieving this is to have the non-alliance companies believe and know that they are part of the 'team' and that their role is appreciated. The alliance members should give some careful thought to measures that might be taken to reinforce and sustain this aspect.

Example. Several alliances have held 'suppliers' days' at regular intervals or to mark key achievements and milestones on the project. At these meetings contributions can be publicly acknowledged. Others have seen that maintaining regular contact and exchanges between the senior management of parties has paid dividends.

11.3 Relationships with external authorities

Many, if not most, capital projects directly involve one or several government or local authority bodies, as well as relevant statutory authorities. It is safe to assert that the way in which these bodies are approached and the relationships that are developed with them will impact on the execution of the project and its ultimate outcome. Almost certainly there will be a primary focus on minimising any potentially adverse effects on cost and schedule. However, this can be regarded as being a somewhat negative approach, and the potential of good relationships with external authorities to add to the value of the project should neither be overlooked nor underestimated.

To have the most beneficial impact the owner should address this issue at the earliest possible stage of the planned development, and develop a strategy and implementation plan focused on developing effective and constructive relationships with all the external bodies that will be involved throughout the proposed development. Underpinning all this should be a willingness and, indeed, determination to approach all external authorities in a positive, open-minded and constructive way, with a view to finding and agreeing solutions that meet the requirements and objectives of all sides.

11.4 Relationships with external organisations and individuals

The impact that external organisations and individuals who do not have a direct involvement in a project can have on a project is frequently evident. An example of this is the disruption that occurs on construction sites as a result of direct action by either pressure groups and/or individuals. As with external authorities, there may be a tendency to approach such issues from a negative point of view, but again a more open-minded and constructive approach may pay large dividends.

In any case, the prudent company should give serious attention to these matters and develop and implement a well thought out strategy and action plan. This should be aimed at gaining positive support for their proposed development and minimising or eliminating the potential for adverse impacts on the development at all its stages.

Bibliography

Associated General Contractors of America (1992). *Partnering: A Concept for Success*. AGC, Washington, DC.

Bennett, J. and Jayes, S. (1998).*The Seven Pillars of Partnering: A Guide to Second Generation Partnering*. University of Reading, Reading.

Bennett, J., Ingram, I. and Jayes, S. (1996). *Partnering for Construction*. Construction Industry Board Working Group 12, London.

Construction Industry Board, Working Group 12 (1997). *Partnering in the Team*. Construction Industry Board, London (partnering video).

Construction Industry Institute (1991). *In Search of Partnering Excellence*. Construction Industry Institute, Austin, TX.

Construction Industry Institute (1994). *Partnering: Strategic Alliances: Cost Savings*. Construction Industry Institute, Austin, TX.

Construction Industry Institute (1994). *Team Building and Project Partnering*. Construction Industry Institute, Austin, TX.

Construction Industry Institute (1996). *The Partnering Process – Its Benefits, Implementation and Measure*. Construction Industry Institute, Austin, TX.

Construction Industry Institute (1997). *Partnering Toolkit*. Construction Industry Institute, Austin, TX.

Critchlow, J. (1998). *Making Partnering Work in the Construction Industry*. Chandos, Oxford.)

Drury, A. (2000). *First Steps in Partnering*. National Housing Federation, London.

European Construction Institute (1997). *Partnering in the Public Sector : A Toolkit for the Implementation of Post Award, Project Specific Partnering on Construction Projects*. ECI, Loughborough.

European Construction Institute Benchmarking Working Group (in preparation). *Risk Management – Value Enhancement Practice*. ECI, Loughborough.

Hellard, R.B. (1995). *Project Partnering: Principle and Practice*. Thomas Telford, London.

Loraine, B. and Williams, I. (2000). *Partnering in the Social Housing Sector*. Thomas Telford, London.

National Economic Development Council Construction Industry Sector Group (1991). *Partnering: Contracting Without Conflict.* NEDC, London.

Partnering Task Force of the Reading Construction Forum (1995). *Trusting the Team: Best Practice Guide to Partnering in Construction..* The Centre for Strategic Studies in Construction, Reading Construction Forum, Reading.

Glossary of terms

adversarialism The conflict encouraged by so-called 'traditional' contracts that force parties primarily to protect their own position irrespective of the end result for the owner or end user.

alignment, alignment process The process by which a group of people, from different companies and/or different departments in a single company, reach agreement on and share a set of common goals and values directed at achieving the project's aims.

alliance, alliancing A form of partnering on a specific project in which a financial incentive scheme links the rewards of each of the alliance members to specified and agreed overall project outcomes and in which all aspects of the arrangement are incorporated in legally binding contracts.

alliance agreement A legally binding contract entered into by the owner and all other member companies in an alliance. It sets out *inter alia* the objectives of the alliance, the details of the alliance financial incentive scheme and the principles that the parties have agreed will govern their working relationships.

alliance board A group of senior managers representing each of the companies participating in an alliance and who are not involved in the day-to-day management of the project. Normally the alliance board does not have any executive authority. Its prime purpose is to provide guidance and support to the owner, other member companies in the alliance and the project team that is responsible and accountable for the management of the project.

alliance financial incentive scheme A scheme incorporated in an alliance agreement to measure the actual performance of the alliance in executing a project against predetermined and agreed performance criteria and performance criteria targets and thereby determine gainshare.

alliance partner(s) This term is used in this book to denote the contractor members of an alliance.

behaviours The way in which people and organisations involved in a project react, one to the other, when dealing with project-related issues and how they react in general to what is going on around them, especially how they cope with changes and uncertainties.

beneficial operation, beneficial use The point at which the product of a construction project begins to produce revenue or other economic benefit to the owner. A device used in an alliance agreement to define project completion for the purposes of the financial incentive scheme.

cap A limit placed on the financial liability of alliance members (other than the owner) resulting from the operation of the alliance financial incentive scheme.

contingency A sum of money included in estimates to cover uncertainties and risks associated with executing a project.

contractor This term is used in a general sense in this book to denote any company or organisation (including consulting engineers) that contracts with an owner company.

excluded risk A risk against which the members of an alliance (other than the owner) are protected in respect of the alliance financial incentive scheme.

expected value outcome The most likely cost of a project in statistical terms, derived from a probabilistic risk analysis.

facilitator At the lowest level of meaning this is a person that a group entrusts with the task of helping them reach a pre-agreed objective, usually at a single meeting. There is, however, a higher type of facilitation, the purpose of which is to open up the participants and individuals to new ways of thinking which will aid them in realising a higher potential for contributing to achieving their objectives.

final cost The actual cost of a project calculated in accordance with the provisions contained in an alliance agreement.

gainshare The sum(s) of money to be paid as a result of the operation of an alliance financial incentive scheme (sometimes referred to as the risk/reward scheme) either by the owner to the other alliance member companies, or vice versa.

integrated team A team composed of personnel from different companies working together on a single project. Individual team members may be led or managed by personnel from a company other than their own.

joint venture   A relationship (usually contractual) formed between two or more contractors and/or suppliers to undertake a project on behalf of an owner.

life-cycle cost   The total cost to an owner of designing, constructing, operating and maintaining a facility throughout its economic working life.

partner   A member of an alliance or partnering arrangement.

partnering, partnering arrangement   An arrangement between two or more companies or organisations, one of which is the owner, which is intended to improve performance in the delivery of a project through achieving high levels of cooperation and collaboration between the parties. The specific aspects of the partnering arrangement are usually embodied in a non-legally-binding partnering charter.

partnering charter   A document signed by parties to a partnering arrangement. *Inter alia*, most partnering charters include a list of objectives and behavioural requirements. Charters are most usually not legally binding.

partnership   Under many legal jurisdictions (e.g. the UK) the term 'partnership' has specific legal connotations, including the inference of joint and several liability when one of the parties to a partnership makes a commitment to a third person.

peer group   A group of people of broadly similar backgrounds, skills, interests and expertise.

performance criteria   The criteria (e.g. capital cost, schedule) that form the basis of an alliance financial incentive scheme.

performance criteria target   The mutually agreed target for a performance criterion against which actual performance will be measured and gainshare calculated in accordance with the alliance financial incentive scheme.

principles   A set of rules mutually agreed by the members of an alliance and incorporated in the alliance agreement to govern and guide the way in which they will conduct their relationship with each other.

procurement (or supply) chain   A term used to denote all parties who are directly involved in delivering a project from the owner, through consultants and contractors, vendors of equipment and bulk materials and every party involved in its construction.

project Any construction or construction-related project undertaken to achieve a specific objective and which has a specific end-date. Projects can range from large new capital works to relatively small modifications to existing facilities.

project alliance leadership team A group composed of the senior project representative (project manager) of each of the member companies of an alliance that *inter alia* is charged with ensuring that the agreed alliance principles are applied at the project-team level.

project intent A device used in an alliance agreement to control the circumstances in which performance criteria targets can be changed.

project-specific partnering, project-specific alliancing The application of partnering or alliancing for the purpose of undertaking a single project.

sanction estimate The cost estimate on which an owner bases his decision to approve the project and determine the sum of money he will allocate for the project execution.

stretch target A target that is beyond that which historical data suggest is possible.

target cost Where cost is a performance criterion, the target cost is the mutually agreed cost against which actual cost performance will be measured as part of the alliance financial incentive scheme.

traditional contracting A term is used to denote contracting practices and forms of contract other than partnering or alliancing.

win–win relationship A relationship whereby all parties benefit from a common project success.

works contract A contract between an owner and an individual alliance member that *inter alia* defines the services to be provided by the alliance member, and establishes the rights and obligations of the parties and the commercial terms that apply in respect of the provision of the services.

workshop A meeting or gathering with the intent of meeting specified objectives. Workshops are often treated as an off-line event for the participants, since the desired outcomes are usually not achievable in the normal course of business.

Appendix 1

Disputes avoidance and disputes resolution

Dispute avoidance

Despite everyone's best endeavours, issues will arise on projects which, unless treated speedily, have the potential to deteriorate into damaging disputes. Such issues usually arise because of poor communication, lack of clarity in scope or specification, changes in scope, inadequate performance, etc. Most of these can be avoided by close attention at the outset of the project, but some are unpredictable and the task is to address these issues before attitudes harden, relationships deteriorate and a full-blown dispute arises. This is the essence of disputes avoidance.

Ideally, such issues should be dealt with speedily and as close to their source as possible. There are some simple principles that should be obeyed. They include:

■ recognise potential problems, avoidance is more cost-effective than resolution
■ address problems early and quickly, they are easier to deal with
■ do not ignore problems, or conceal them, they will only fester
■ seek to resolve problems, not assign blame
■ resolve issues as close to their source as possible.

Virtually all alliance projects will have an alliance board comprising representatives of the parties to the alliancing arrangement. The board will keep all such issues under review and, as a matter of routine, attempt to find harmonious solutions informally through discussion or even negotiation. The alliance board, or a designated panel of the board, may also represent a stage in a semi-formal disputes avoidance procedure, either by requiring all contentious issues to be reported directly to them or by placing themselves at some point within a disputes avoidance ladder.

The ladder is a structured process for the resolution of issues within a given time frame. In accordance with the principle that issues should be resolved as early as possible and as near to their source as possible, the ladder will typically identify the level at which the issue should be discussed and the time frame during which it should be resolved at each level. For example:

■ supervisor level – within 24 hours
■ project manager level – within 2 days

■ alliance board level – within 1 week
■ executive level – within 2 weeks.

Issues not settled during these processes will probably be the subject of a dispute resolution process. However, it should be remembered that issues can be resolved by negotiation at any time, and that in all cases work should continue pending resolution.

Dispute resolution

It is highly desirable that issues and problems should be resolved through the informal dispute avoidance procedure. However, where this fails there is usually recourse to a dispute resolution process, which may be specified either in the contract or in the alliance agreement. It is also desirable and entirely within the spirit of alliancing that the avoidance procedure should be exhausted before the resolution procedure is invoked. However, it is unlikely that this will be mandatory.

The cost, time and sheer acrimony of litigation has led to the development of alternative approaches to dispute resolution. There are numerous Alternative Dispute Resolution (ADR) processes available. Almost any method of resolving disputes that does not involve arbitration or litigation would fall into this category. However, while their use is increasing in construction, the enforceability of their determinations varies between countries, and final resort may still be made to litigation. Despite this, disputes can be resolved quickly using ADR methods. The particular method to be used should be stipulated in the contract. The most important of these ADR methods are described below.

Dispute review board

Perhaps the most appropriate ADR method for alliance projects, particularly in the construction industry, for which it was devised, is the Disputes Review Board (DRB). Like the avoidance procedures, it attempts to resolve the issues 'on site'.

There are several DRB models available, but typically the board comprises three members. One member is chosen by the owner, and one by the contractor. Together they choose the third member, who acts as the chairman. Members should have complementary expertise and must be available at short notice to resolve disputes.

The DRB is a standing body. Provision for its operation should be in the contract and it should be set up at the very beginning of the project. Its members are made familiar with the project and are supplied, on a regular basis, with information such as progress reports, plans and specifications. They may also make periodic visits to site.

In the event of a dispute each party is afforded an opportunity to present to the board, in the presence of the other, information that it thinks relevant to the dispute. The board can also conduct its own investigation. However, under no circumstances can the board communicate with one party in the absence of the other. A decision should be reached quickly, without interrupting work on the project. DRBs can be used in an advisory or binding adjudication-type capacity. However, even if the decision is not binding it is usually accepted, since the DRB's recommendations would normally be used as evidence in any subsequent arbitration or litigation. There is also a possibility that, because of the non-legal standing of the board, its adjudicated decision may be questioned and appealed against.

A standing DRB can be very costly and is only really appropriate for larger projects or contracts. On smaller projects a single disputes review advisor might be appointed, whose decision is implemented even though it might be subsequently overturned in court. This approach, however, is not dissimilar to adjudication, which is another ADR method.

Adjudication

Where this is the preferred dispute resolution method, the appointment of the adjudicator, who should be an independent third party, should constitute part of the contract negotiation. The intention of this method is that the adjudicator should make a speedy decision, which must be complied with but which will, if one party is dissatisfied, be open to review in formal proceedings in due course.

A procedure for the election of adjudicators and the time frames within which adjudication should proceed should also be set out in the contract. An example of this procedure is set out in Section 108 of the UK Housing Grant Construction and Regeneration Act. Under this Section, any contract must now contain:

■ a provision for a party to give notice of their intention to refer a dispute to adjudication
■ a timetable for the referral of the dispute to the other party within 7 days of the notice
■ a 28-day period for decision-making
■ a provision for an extension of time of up to 14 days if agreed by the parties.

The adjudication decision should be written and expressed to be final and binding unless written notice to the contrary is given within a specified number of days of the decision being given to the parties. It should in any case be binding until the completion of the works. After completion the dispute can be referred to arbitration or to the courts, providing that notice is given within the time frame set out in the contract.

Under the UK Act, adjudication can be introduced at any time (i.e. regardless of whatever disputes resolution process is underway), providing that the agreed procedure is followed. However, because of the tight timetable imposed by the Act there can be difficulty in combining it with other forms of dispute resolution process that might be more appropriate to alliancing arrangements.

Mediation

Mediation is a technique favoured in many countries. A neutral mediator is appointed by the parties to investigate the causes of the dispute and to facilitate an acceptable solution. It is voluntary, non-binding (unless agreed by the parties) and relatively informal.

Each party to the dispute is represented by an individual who must be sufficiently senior to have the authority to settle on behalf of his organisation. The mediator should clearly be impartial and be respected by both parties. His role is purely facilitative; he has no authority to make any sort of determination. By a process of listening, counselling, suggesting and persuading, he helps the parties themselves to arrive at an amicable solution and settlement.

There are no hard and fast rules for a mediation process. The mediator clearly needs to familiarise himself with the facts and request documentation from and seek meetings with each side. Equality of treatment, impartiality and openness are the guiding principles. While the process is informal, it is not a soft option. Mediation will only work if:

- both sides are well prepared
- both sides are willing to compromise
- both sides are honest with themselves as to the merits of their position
- the mediator is competent
- each party is represented by a person who has authority to reach a compromise.

Mediation does not affect the parties' recourse to the courts in the event that it fails, but it has often been found to be most successful if one of the parties has started down the path to litigation.

Other ADR processes

There are several other ADR processes, including: Expert Determination, MedArb, Mini-trial, Rent a Judge, etc. Greater detail can be obtained from the Centre for Dispute Resolution (CEDR), Princes House, 95 Gresham Street, London EC2V 7NA.

Appendix 2

Targets in the context of an alliance

Setting and articulating targets for performance which are explicitly quantified rather than expressed in general terms has been shown to be a valuable tool in achieving performance improvements.

Having the targets quantified has several important aspects, including:

- the business aspirations are clearly set out and a context and framework for achieving and maintaining competitive advantage is established
- actual performance against desired performance can easily be measured
- an explicit context for conducting activities and decision-making is provided.

Quantified performance targets have an equally significant importance in regard to capital projects, both from the point of view the owner making investment decisions and in terms of the final delivery of the project.

However, various performance criteria or targets may be used and at different stages of a project, and difficulties have been experienced through a failure to distinguish between different types of target and the consequences of failure to achieve them. Creating and retaining distinctions in regard to the different targets in the context of an alliance is particularly important.

Targets

In an alliance capital project there will usually be three principal sets of targets that need to be distinguished and, more importantly, kept distinct:

- targets relating to the economic viability of the project – investment targets
- targets incorporated within the alliance agreement – performance criteria targets
- targets for the actual execution and delivery of the project – delivery targets.

Investment targets will almost always have no contractual significance, and the consequence of failure to meet them may simply be a decision by the owner not to proceed with the project and thus the loss of potential work for the contractors.

Performance criteria targets are contractual and are used to determine the ultimate remuneration of the parties in the alliance. The consequence of beating the targets will be direct financial rewards to the contractor members of the alliance and more economic asset for the owner. A failure to meet the targets will have the opposite impact.

Delivery targets (sometimes referred to as *stretch targets*) are related to achieving performance that exceeds the performance targets stated in the alliance agreement. They are usually (and most powerfully) set by the project team itself and it is vital to recognise that they have no contractual significance.

It is equally important to recognise that it is not intended that success or failure of the project team in respect of their delivery targets will have any direct consequences either for the team or the individual members. Rewards or sanctions for the team and the individuals on it will usually be governed by the remuneration and performance policies of the individual companies.

Appendix 3

Examples of project intents

Example 1

The project intent comprises the following parameters:

General

Overall objective

The design, procurement, precommissioning and commissioning of a cross-country pipeline (CCP) to carry high-pressure ethylene. The ethylene quality will be between M1 and M2 specification, as presently conveyed in the existing 10-feet diameter A to B Pipeline Project (ABPP).

Location

The CCP will commence at a tie-in to the off-take site (OTS) at [*location of off-take site*] and terminate at the boundary of the ethylene reception facility (ERF) located within the fence line of [*location of reception facility*].

The pipeline is approximately [*length*], and follows the route submitted to the DTI in the Pipeline Construction Authorisation request of [*date*].
See: *Letter reference* _____

Design data

Pipeline diameter (nom.)	12 feet
Pipeline depth of cover (min.)	1100 mm
Operating pressure (max.)	95 barg
Operating pressure (min)	55 barg
Design pressure	102 barg
Operating flow rate (max.)	22.9 te/h
Operating flow rate (min)	3.7 te/h
Design flow rate (future upgrade)	130.0 te/h
Block valve sites (incl. intermediate pigging station)	9 No.

Custody transfer metering, filtration (if required), emergency shutdown and isolation valve, temporary pigging, and future tie-in facilities will be provided at the OTS. Similar facilities will be provided at the ERF, but the metering will be required for integrity monitoring purposes only.

No permanent pigging facilities will be provided, but the pipeline will be designed to be pigged both during construction, and also in operation if required. Bend radii, internal diameters and layouts will be sized to allow inspection by the PII Intelligence Pig.

Excluded risks

Changes in legislation

A variation occasioned by a change in statutory requirements, any regulations issued pursuant thereto, guidance notes issued by official agencies in respect of such requirements of regulations or any interpretation by official agencies of such requirements, regulations or guidance notes relating to the design of the CCP facilities from those in force at 7 May 199X shall be deemed to be a change to the project intent for the purposes of this Agreement.

Access

The company will ensure free access to the land commensurate with the two-season construction period.

Example B

Location and layout

The ABC Project will be located to the north of the existing facilities on a largely filled and level plot and the new facilities will be arranged as shown on the attached general plot plan.

Technology

The ABC plant will be designed to use XYZ's BB technology with direct injection supported XX catalyst and a high-efficiency reactor using pentane condensation.

Capacity

The ABC plant will be designed as a swing HDPE/C4LLDPE plant with a capacity of 200 Kte/a. The design grades and rates associated with this capacity will be:

| Product A | 25 te/h | design grade XX |
| Product B | 30 te/h | design grade YY |

Degassing and powder-handling equipment will be designed for a future nominal capacity of 300 Kte/a which will be achieved from using ZZZ technology.

Extrusion capability will be circa 15% above the maximum production rate.

Excluded risks

Changes in legislation

A variation occasioned by a change in 'Country' statutory requirements, any regulations issued pursuant thereto, decrees or guidance notes issued by official agencies in respect of such requirements or regulations or any reinterpretation by Indonesian official agencies of such requirements, regulations, decrees or guidance notes relating to the design of the ABC Project from those in force at 15 January 1996 shall be deemed to be a change to the PROJECT INTENT for the purposes of Subclause 14.1 of this AGREEMENT but the requirements of Clause 14 thereof still apply.

Example C

1. The XYZ Project will be located to the south of B's ABC Project which in turn will be located to the south of the existing CCC plant and will be arranged as shown on the attached general plot plan within the battery limits also as shown on the general plot plan on Attachment 1 to this Appendix.
2. On completion the XYZ plant will have a nominal production capacity of X hundred thousand tonnes per annum of [*type of product*] based on the Grade Slate shown in Attachment 2 to this Appendix and using raw materials to the specifications detailed in Attachment 3 to this Appendix.
3. The XYZ plant will be designed to utilise A's ABC Technology with direct injection supported VVV catalyst and high productivity using hexene-1 as the co-monomer as defined in Attachment 4 to this Appendix.
4. The XYZ plant will be designed for continuous plant operation at the following design rates and grades:

LL6208	41 tonne/h	Density 920 kg/m^3; melt index 0.75
LL6130	35 tonne/h	Density 918 kg/m^3; melt index 3.00.

5. The pelletised product will be conveyed by pipeline to silos and dispatch facilities located outside the battery limits (OSBL).
6. The XYZ plant will be designed to have an operating life of 20 years.
7. The XYZ plant will be designed to operate for 3 years before its first planned major shutdown.
8. The XYZ plant will be designed to have an extrusion capacity circa 10% above the production rates detailed in paragraph 4 above of this Appendix.
9. Spares will be installed for pumps in continuous operation and for conveying blowers with common spares being used where appropriate on dualled streams/trains.
10. Space provision will be made within the XYZ plant layout to accommodate a future second catalyst injection train to use UUU super strength (ss) or metalocene catalyst.

Excluded risks

11. In the event that Beneficial Operation cannot be achieved due to the failure of A's ABC technology then this will be deemed to be a change to the Project Intent for the purposes of this Agreement.

12. The Company shall be responsible for proving the following in sufficient quantities such that the achievement of Beneficial Operation by the Target Beneficial Operation Date shall not be prejudiced:

     (a) The following utilities:

     - steam at high and medium pressure
     - high purity nitrogen at high pressure
     - standard purity nitrogen
     - towns water
     - fire water
     - electrical power at 33 kV
     - instrument air
     - permanent waste water treatment.

     (b) The OSBL facilities for receiving and despatching pelletised production.

     Any failure to provide any of the above which directly delays achievement of beneficial operation will be deemed to be a change to the project intent for the purposes of this Agreement.

13. In the event that the Company requests any the following modifications and/or additions:

     (a) on or before the date specified against each then this will be deemed to be a change to the project intent for the purposes of this Agreement provided that only amendments to the Alliance Cost Estimate shall be considered; *or*

     (b) after the date specified against each then this will be deemed to be a change to the project intent for the purposes of this Agreement

Additional reagent systems	end September 199X
Hexane storage and injection system	end September 199X
Talc silo and feeders	end August 199X
MFM catalyst flow meters	end September 199X
TNPP provision	end June 199X
Ethylene let down system	end May 199X
Feedstock preparation area (including ethylene and hexene)	end March 199X

14. In the event that the Company requests any of the following modifications after the date specified against each then this will be deemed to be a change to the project intent for the purposes of this Agreement:

   ■ Catalyst injection system   end June 199X
   ■ High productivity nozzles (6 nozzle system instead of 4) end June 199X

15. A change in statutory requirements, any regulations issued pursuant thereto, decrees or guidance notes issued by official agencies in respect of such requirements or regulations relating to the design of the XYZ plant from those in force at 1 January 199X shall be deemed to be a change to the project intent for the purposes of this Agreement.
   For the avoidance of doubt, the provisions of this Paragraph 15 shall not apply to such changes that had been announced prior to 1 January 199X but were not due to be promulgated until after 1 January 199X.

16. In the event that the Company unilaterally changes the Target Beneficial Operation date then such change shall be deemed to be a change to the project intent for the purposes of this Agreement.